T0354472

80 Years of Memories of Life in Hawai'i and Beyond

Biographical Stories About Life from 1929 to 2013

William Harrison Wright, Jr.

Order this book online at www.trafford.com
or email orders@trafford.com

Most Trafford titles are also available at major online book retailers.

Print information available on the last page.

ISBN: 978-1-4907-7175-5 (sc)
ISBN: 978-1-4907-7176-2 (hc)
ISBN: 978-1-4907-7177-9 (e)

Library of Congress Control Number: 2016904742

Trafford rev. 12/21/2016

www.trafford.com
North America & international
toll-free: 1 888 232 4444 (USA & Canada)
fax: 812 355 4082

CONTENTS

• • • • • • • •●●● ●●●● • • • • • •

PREFACE

A number of years ago Beverly Kapualehuanani and Kathleen Pualani, my two daughters, wanted to know more about what it was like living in Hawai'i, what sort of games I played when I was a youngster, and what it was like living on Kaua'i, the fourth largest island in the Hawaiian Archipelago. "Tell us about the attack on Pearl Harbor and Hickam Field on December 7, 1941," they said.

While writing about Pearl Harbor and the events that took place that fateful day, I was reminded of the many beautiful stories my mother and father told me, stories about what it was like when they were young. Many of those stories, I recall, were hilarious! With that thought in mind, I felt others might enjoy stories of what it was like growing up in a town with a population of 1500 people, a town where people of different cultural lifestyles came together, a town surrounded by sugarcane fields and a sugar mill that was part of the economy of Hawai'i during the 1930s. I also thought my stories would be more entertaining if I inserted some humor now and then.

I am indebted to my daughters for their many questions about my life, which eventually led me to write these autobiographical tales. But just as importantly, it is for my descendants whom I will never know.

With a deep sense of humility, these autobiographical sketches are dedicated to my daughters, Kathleen Pualani and Beverly Kapualehuanani; to my stepdaughters, Shelley Lynne (Fletcher) Temple and Angelica Renee Fletcher; and to Gail Katherine (Hatton), my friend, my companion, and my wife, who persistently encouraged me to pursue this adventure in writing. I must also include in this dedication my granddaughters Kemelia (Keith) Mileaf, Lindsay Fox and Kate Fox along with step-granddaughters Shannon (Jarrell) Apsey, Emily (Jarrell) Smith, Rebekah Jarrell, Malorie Lane, Chelsea Lane and Alexis (Russell) Nolasco-Reyes.

To those whose names I included in this autobiography, I hope they will understand how instrumental they were in the writing of my memoirs. Without them, this book would not have been possible. Believe me, it's a miracle I've gotten this far!

PROLOGUE

· · · · · · ● ● ● ● · · · · · ·

Several underlying factors led to the attack on Pearl Harbor. After Japan invaded Manchuria (1931), the League of Nations (1933) condemned the Japanese for their aggressive action, which prompted their delegation to walk out of the organization. Ignoring all previous agreements, the Japanese government (1936) embarked on a massive expansion of its naval force. In December 1937, while escorting American oil tankers along the Yangtze River, Japanese aircraft sank the USS *Panay*. Although there was no retaliation, the United States State Department made a strong protest. In 1938 Japan closed its Open Door policy, prompting the United States to renounce its trade treaty with Japan and place an embargo on metal exports to Japan. In May 1940, with tensions rising throughout the Pacific, Pearl Harbor became the main Pacific base for the United States fleet. In July 1941, the United States placed an embargo on all strategic exports to Japan and froze Japan's assets in the United States.

Historians tell us the attack on Pearl Harbor was timed to occur after the Japanese ambassadors presented their declaration of war to the Secretary of State, the Honorable Cordell Hull. It must have been a seriously embarrassing moment for Japan's Ambassador Kurusu to learn that while he was waiting in another room to be acknowledged by the secretary of state, Japanese aircraft had already bombed and strafed military bases on O'ahu.

On December 8, 1941, the president of the United States, Franklin Delano Roosevelt, speaking to members of the House of Representative and the Senate, declared that a war existed between the United States of America and the Japanese Empire. World War II was now a fact!

In August 1940, at an elevation of 750 feet above sea level, a new campus with six dormitories on Kapalama Heights opened its doors for students enrolled at the Kamehameha School for Boys. From this campus, looking south, was the world-famous Diamond Head, and as the eyes moved westward, there was a sweeping view of a calm Pacific Ocean. Below the campus was the city of Honolulu with its tallest structure, a ten-story building called Aloha Tower, welcoming ships of all nations into its peaceful harbor. Adjacent to Honolulu Harbor was Hickam Army Airfield of which John Rogers Airport, Honolulu's airfield, was a part. Northwest of this airfield was Pearl Harbor where the Pacific Naval Command had its many warships anchored as a peacetime navy. Looking beyond Pearl Harbor was the Wai'ainae mountain range on the left and Ko'olau mountain range on the right. Between these two landmasses was a large agricultural area occupied by the Waipahu Sugar Plantation and farther away, with binoculars, pineapple fields owned by the Dole Pineapple Company could be seen from the newly opened Kamehameha School campus. Out of sight but at the base of the Wai'ainae Mountain Range was a small village, Wahiawa, where Schofield Barracks was located, a military installation that was one of the largest maintained by the United States Army.

Adjacent to Schofield Barracks was Wheeler Field where the US Army Air Corps housed its fighter squadrons. This was the scene as viewed from the campus on December 7, 1941.

From this campus students and faculty members had a clear view of the attack on Pearl Harbor and Hickam Field. Initially, no one on the campus was aware or afraid of what was happening until radio announcers on stations KGU and KGMB told listeners, "This is the real McCoy! Japanese planes are attacking Pearl Harbor and Hickam Field; all military personnel report to your stations immediately!" Included in this announcement was the order for civilians to take cover.

Kamehameha Students in World War II gives an eyewitness account of the attack on Pearl Harbor and Hickam Field as we saw it, the initial reactions that took place, and how students at Kamehameha contributed to the war effort.

In November 2009, I spoke to Janet Zisk, archivist for the Kamehameha School, and showed her a sample of my writing. After reading the sample, she said, "No one from the school who saw the attack submitted an eyewitness account of this event. Your book should be included in our archives." One copy of this booklet was given to Janet Zisk and an additional five copies were presented to Midkiff Learning Center at Kamehameha.

It was never my intention to publish my account of this historical event because it was written primarily for my daughters, family members, and other individuals who might have an interest in reading how Kamehameha students actually participated in World War II.

In memory of the Kamehameha students who served their country during World War II, this booklet is humbly dedicated.

RECOLLECTIONS OF YESTERYEAR (1931-2012)

• • • • • • • ● ● ● ● ● • • • • • •

<u>1931</u> (two years old). From Kaua'i my mother and I sailed to Honolulu on the SS *Waialeale* to see my grandmother who was very ill. I recall seeing my grandmother lying in her bed; her wrinkled face and hands frightened me.

<u>1931</u> (two years old). While in Honolulu, we visited my aunt Rose, my mother's sister, who took care of me for almost a year after I was born. I remember being bored listening to the two women talking, so I asked my mother if I could go outside. Sitting on the top step of the front porch, I watched mynah birds in the trees and on the ground. This was much more interesting than listening to two ladies chatting.

<u>1933</u> (4½ years old). While my parents were vacationing on the mainland and seeing the World's Fair in Chicago, I stayed with my aunt Angela, my father's sister, who lived in Waimea Valley on Kaua'i, not too far from the Menehune Ditch. My cousin, Allen Gouveia, took a liking to me. He let me sit on his lap so he could teach me how to play his guitar. Because my fingers were too small to reach across the neck of the guitar, he fingered the chords while I strummed.

Allen created a toy telephone for me by stretching one hundred feet of copper wire and attaching tin cans at each end. One can was on the porch of the house; the other can was on a hook nailed to a mango tree four feet off the ground, just high enough for me to grasp it so we could have a "telephone" conversation. He also made a "crystal" radio hooked to earphones and let me listen to people talking to each other. He never did this for his younger brother, Kenneth, who was a year older than me.

Allen made a boat by attaching two corrugated tin roofing slabs to a wooden stick on one end that became the bow and a thin flat board on the other end as the stern of the craft. He gathered road rocks that had tar on them and heated the rocks until the tar melted to produce enough of a gooey, sticky substance. This was his sealant for the boat. He used his boat to cross the Waimea River about 175 feet from one shore to the other. The river was just fifty yards from the house. Allen spent a lot of time with me that summer letting me stir the sticky tar into a gooey mess, explaining how and why my telephone worked, and teaching me songs a 4½-year-old might like. Allen was nine years old.

Before leaving Hawai'i, my father purchased a new automobile that he would pick up in Detroit, drive to San Francisco, and then ship to Kaua'i. Unlike today's vehicles, this car had no trunk, but it did have a metal grill that could be pulled down so suitcases or other gear could be attached to it.

Buick Limo

<u>1934</u> (five years old). I watched a bumblebee f lying in and out of a hole in a wood fence along the front yard of our house in Kekaha. Was this my first lesson in the field of entomology?

1935 (six years old). While visiting the Thurston family in Honolulu,

Pan American Clipper

Uncle Paul Thurston took Charlie (my cousin) and me to Pearl Harbor to see the Pan American Clipper arriving on its history-making inaugural flight. This flight originated from Alameda, California, on Wednesday at 3:00 p.m. guided by a radio beacon from Mokapu Point, located at Kane'ohe Naval Air Station. Passengers sleeping in their individual cabins (like a Pullman roomette on a train) were awakened so they could view Maui and the Moloka'i shoreline before arriving in Honolulu at 9:00 a.m. Thursday. After an overnight visit to O'ahu, this journey continued northwest toward Kaua'i and Ni'ihau before landing in a lagoon at Midway Atoll nine hours later. After another overnight stop, the flight was off to Wake Island, Guam, and its final destination, Manila Bay, Philippine Islands. At approximately two hundred miles per hour, this flight logged more than thirty hours of flying time.

1935 (six years old). I started first grade at Kekaha Elementary School in September and completed second grade in June 1936.

1938 (nine years old). I went to fourth grade at Lincoln Elementary School in Honolulu.

1939 (ten years old). My first airplane ride was from Honolulu to Kaua'i on an Inter-Island Airways (Hawaiian Airlines) nineteen-passenger Sikorsky S-43 seaplane. The flight from John Rogers

Airport (Honolulu International) to Port Allen, Kaua'i, a distance of approximately 130 miles, took one hour.

Sikorsky S-43 preserved at Pima Air & Space Museum, Tucson AZ

1940 (eleven years old). The new campus for students entering Kamehameha School for Boys opened on Kapalama Heights in Honolulu. Our class (1946) was the first group to start and complete its education entirely at the new campus.

1941 (eleven years old). On December 7, watching the attack on Pearl Harbor and Hickam Field was awesome and spectacular. My booklet *Kamehameha Students During World War II* is an eyewitness account of the event.

1946 (seventeen). After graduating from Kamehameha, I spent the next school year (1946–47) at Farrington High School to obtain additional math and science credits (second year algebra, trigonometry, and physics) for my high school record.

1947 (eighteen). My first trip to the US mainland was on Matson Navigation's SS *Matsonia*. We left Honolulu on August 3 and arrived in Los Angeles (Wilmington Harbor) four and half days later. There were 680 passengers when we left Honolulu, most of whom were students heading back to their colleges and universities. Half of them disembarked in Los Angeles. The rest of the passengers, most of them students, continued on to San Francisco for colleges in northern

California, Oregon, and Washington. The *Matsonia* left Los Angeles at 6:00 p.m. the following evening and arrived in San Francisco the next morning at 11:30 a.m.

Because this was an overnight stopover in Los Angeles, four of us took a commuter train from Wilmington Harbor to downtown Los Angeles and stayed at a small hotel on Fourth Street called The Alexander. We returned to the ship the next day on a commuter train but stopped just long enough to purchase a twenty-four-pound watermelon. Four of us chipped in twelve cents each, hopped on the next train, and continued on to Wilmington Harbor to board our ship. One of the guys managed to get a knife from the ship's kitchen. Spreading a towel on the deck, we gorged ourselves on the fruit.

There were two celebrities on this trip, musician and composer Irving Berlin, and actor George Brent. During the evening, when Irving Berlin sat at a piano, passengers bombarded him with requests to play popular tunes. A favorite was "Remember Pearl Harbor" written shortly after the December seventh attack. George Brent was rarely seen throughout the voyage, but after the ship docked in Wilmington, I noticed he was helped off the ship toward the stern of the vessel via the crew's gangplank. Several passengers remarked that the actor was constantly inebriated.

Sixty years later (2009), while searching Google for general information for my autobiography, I saw the passenger list for the SS *Matsonia* and discovered the Lindsay Faye family also had been on that voyage. During the five days of sailing, I never ran across them on the ship. I did not see Mary and Linda on the manifest but assume they, too, were on their way to California. Note: Lindsay A. Faye, Sr. was a manager of the Kekaha Sugar Company. His family and mine were friends and neighbors.

1948 (nineteen). I worked on a tugboat called *Agnes Foss* that left Honolulu bound for the Pacific Northwest. The trip began May 1 and ended twenty-nine days later in Seattle, Washington. It took twenty-seven days to reach Astoria, Oregon, where one of the two barges we had been towing was taken by a Coast Guard ship and delivered to Portland, Oregon. We had to wait for the tide to move inland before heading up the Columbia River. It was twelve miles from the Columbia Lightship at the mouth of the river to Astoria. We started our trip to Astoria at 6:00 p.m. and arrived at midnight. On our way back to the Pacific, it took only an hour and a half to reach the same distance.

1948 (nineteen). I was impressed with Seattle and its warm, sunny days during that summer, so I enrolled at the University of Washington. When classes started in September so did the constant drizzle. Except for five minutes in October I never saw the sun. When I returned to Hawai'i for Christmas that year, I stayed there.

1949 (twenty). I entered New Mexico Highlands University in Las Vegas, New Mexico, a small college town with a population of about fifteen thousand people, just sixty-five miles from Santa Fe and about 130 miles from New Mexico's largest city, Albuquerque. While listening to a newscast about the World Series baseball game, I was elated to hear that the New York Yankees had beaten the Brooklyn Dodgers by taking the last four games of the series. The Dodgers had defeated the Yankees with three straight wins but just couldn't get another win. The Dodgers could have been World Series champions that year had they been able to win just one more game.

1950 (twenty-one). Because the high altitude in Las Vegas (6,700 feet) was affecting my breathing, the physician at New Mexico Highlands University wrote a letter to my parents in Honolulu suggesting I return to Hawai'i. My flights had me on three airlines: Frontier Airlines operating a DC-3 (Las Vegas to Albuquerque), a tri-tailed TWA Constellation (Albuquerque to Los Angeles), and a DC-4 aircraft to Honolulu operated by United Airlines.

1951 (twenty-two). I was enrolled at the University of Hawai'i when I received a draft notice requiring me to report for induction into the US Army. Having anticipated this might happen, I had already submitted my request for OCS (Officers Candidate School) and was told to report to Schofield Barracks in Honolulu within two weeks. After completing basic infantry training and leadership school at Fort Ord, California, I opted to be discharged in San Diego rather than Honolulu.

1952 (twenty-three). After a short courtship of four months, I married Theresa Sharretts Lindsay, a WAVE stationed at Pearl Harbor. Because enlisted women were not permitted to be married while serving their military tour of duty, she was discharged; we returned to her hometown, Towson, Maryland.

1955 (twenty-six). A friend told me he detected an accent in my speech and asked if everyone in Hawai'i ended their sentences in an upbeat as if they were asking a question. I really didn't know what he was talking about so I ignored the comment. However, when my parents visited me in Maryland, I noticed they had a very distinct accent, and yes, their sentences did end as if they were asking a question!

1962 (thirty-three). Not having seen Hawai'i during the ten years I lived in Maryland, I gathered a group of coworkers to join me in Honolulu. As their tour guide, I was compensated with a round-trip fare. At a half-fare rate, my two daughters accompanied me on their first trip to Hawai'i.

1963. Tragically, my wife Tess, at just thirty-four years of age, passed away leaving two daughters, eight and ten, in the care of a father who lacked parenting skills but had to learn—fast!

1970 (forty-one). When my father passed away, I returned to Honolulu. After seventeen years of fast-paced living in Maryland, I had to adapt to the slow, lackadaisical lifestyle Hawai'i offered. I was bored and longed to return to the mainland. Nine years later my wish came true. Xerox hired my very good friend and future wife Gail as a technician in Honolulu in November 1972. While on a business trip to Maryland, Gail and I got married (May 1974), so when Xerox transferred her to be an instructor at the Xerox Management and Training Center in Leesburg, Virginia (January 1977), I got back to my fast-paced lifestyle.

1979 (fifty). After completing two and a half years at the Leesburg Training Center, my wife was offered a position in San Diego as a field service manager for Xerox; we have been California residents for more than thirty-three years.

1980 (fifty-one). With a background as an engineering writer for Westinghouse in Baltimore, my first job in San Diego was senior editor for DATA Books (a reference manual listing electronic devices specifically designed for electrical engineers). This company is a subsidiary of Mitchell Manuals (auto industry).

1981–83 (fifty-two). After resigning from DATA Books, I decided to pursue further education at San Diego Mira Mar College. My first day of classes was a shocker! Students nineteen to twenty-two years of age thought I was their instructor.

1983 (fifty-four). Following my graduation from Mira Mesa College, I joined General Dynamics as an engineering writer on the cruise missile program.

1984–86 (fifty-five). Rockwell International hired me as a lead writer, Publications Department, for the B-1 bomber project.

2011–2012 (eighty-three). I completed *More Than 80 Years of Memories* in August. Revisions to my autobiography completed in September 2012.

MY OLD FRIEND

· · · · · · · · · ● · · · · · · · ·

   An emigrant from China—from where, what area, what province, what city, what year, I have no idea—he was in Hawai'i on the island of Kaua'i, a wise and kindly old man, soft spoken, always with a smile on his face. His grasp of the English language was limited, but with his fluency in speaking and understanding the Hawaiian language, his command of a Chinese dialect my father haltingly understood, and a few words of other languages thrown into the conversation, we were able to converse in pigeon English, a language familiar to those born and raised in Hawai'i. His name was Apu, and he was our yard man.

Apu's apartment adjacent to garage; door on right is laundry room

1

Apu lived in a small but comfortable studio apartment attached to our garage, about twenty yards from the main house, the same house in which I was born. The year of this story is 1934; I was five years old.

Looking back on those early years, I recall enjoying my visits to Apu's apartment where he always had something good to eat and drink. It wasn't candy or soda pop, but it was almost as good. There was his pot of tea, freshly brewed each morning and kept warm throughout the day in an ancient insulated crock, and when evening approached, it was just cool enough to drink without having to blow steam away from the cup. At the main house we usually had supper around six in the evening. Apu often ate an hour or so later. Once in a while I would eat just enough to satisfy my parents, excuse myself from the table, and run across the backyard to Apu's apartment to join him for dinner. His meals were absolutely scrumptious, at least to my taste buds. I always liked his *hom yee* (salt fish), *kauyuk* (pork pot roast), and *laup cheong* (Chinese sausage), and the way he stir-fried his vegetables in a hot, steaming skillet, with, of course, lots of rice and several cups of tea to complete the evening menu. We didn't have that type of meal in our house too often, so whenever Apu told me what he was going to have for dinner, if it was a meal I liked, I ate sparingly at home.

On his day off, Apu often let me accompany him wherever he was going. One of my favorite outings was to visit his friend Atung, who lived about eight houses from where we lived. I could never understand why Apu insisted I stay outside, but I think it was because I seemed too engrossed and fascinated by the long-stemmed pipe Atung used. I watched him tap what looked like a gummy piece of tobacco into the tiny bowl at the end of his pipe, lighting the wax, slowly inhaling, and then slowly exhaling the sweet-smelling smoke from his lips. It was a pleasant odor, one that I liked. On one of our visits, Atung noticed how much I enjoyed being there and very politely offered me a puff on his pipe. As I entered Atung's hut to reach for the pipe, Apu grabbed my hand and, with a few choice words (in Chinese) to his friend, stomped out of the house. From that moment on, Apu never let me accompany him when he went to visit

Atung. As you can guess, that sweet, spiraling smoke filling the room was opium. I guess Apu felt my visits to his friend's house might get me started on an addiction.

The last time I saw Apu was in December 1948 when I was home from the University of Washington to celebrate Christmas. I found out that he was living in a home for the aged, all of whom were Chinese, and I did not recognize him. With so many Chinese at that home, they all looked alike to me. Perhaps the saddest part was how kindly he had been to me during my early childhood, yet how forgetful I was. It was difficult to carry on a coherent conversation with him; the words and phrases so understandable when I was five years old had been lost to me. I know the visit was a real joy to Apu; I could see his eyes beaming like Christmas tree ornaments. He called me "Willie Boy," the same name he called my father. One of his many phrases was "Kakalina, you likee olongee?" Translated, he was saying, "Carolyn, would you like an orange?" *Kakalina* is the Hawaiian name for Carolyn, my sister's name. Apu must have been close to fifty years old when my father was born (October 1897). Apu was 101 the last time I saw him.

THE CARROTS, WHAT A MARVELOUS VEGETABLE-- THE POWER IT POSSESSES!

· · · · · · · ● ● ● ● ● · · · · ·

The carrot, that wonderful, orange-colored vegetable root sliced into small, bite-sized strips offered as a delicious finger food, is very tasty when dipped in a creamy ranch sauce. The carrot, a vegetable known for its Vitamin A, a vitamin that greatly improves eyesight, is taken from Mother Earth and given to youngsters to make them healthy and strong. Carrots are vital to growing youngsters, or so I was told during one evening meal.

What are vitamins? I couldn't see vitamins, but I could see carrots on my plate and carrots always made me gag. At 4½ years old, I knew what I wanted and what I didn't want. I didn't want carrots!

We had a round dinner table; my mother sat facing my father, I sat to his right, and my sister sat across from me. Most of our evening meals were spent quietly, but on this occasion a mere vegetable, the carrot, became a heated issue of conversation.

Recalling the incident so many, many years ago, I remember my father calling me a "stubborn mule," ordering me not to leave the table until I ate the carrots on my plate.

Our dessert that evening was ice cream, my favorite. I didn't get any because I didn't eat my carrots. Having been ordered to do so, I sat at the dining table when my parents got up and retired to the living room where, as was their custom, my father read the newspaper and my mother did some darning. My sister went of bed. After clearing the dining table, except for the dinner plate sitting in front of me, and cleaning the kitchen, our housemaid announced to my parents that she was ready to go home. I heard my father ask her to turn off the light in the dining room. Although she paused a moment to say something, she, nevertheless, quietly turned, reentered the dining room, and turned off the light on her way to the kitchen.

Sitting at the dining table in the dark room, with tears rolling down my cheeks, I didn't whimper or make sobbing sounds, nor did I eat the carrots on the plate in front of me.

Around 10:30 p.m. I heard my parents getting up from their chairs in the living room. One light went out, then another. Before extinguishing the last light in the living room, my father waited for my mother to turn on the light on the way to their bedroom. Glancing into the dining room, my mother gasped! To my father, she said, "He's still at the table! Poor thing, we forgot all about him!"

"I thought he went to bed," my father replied.

After telling me to go to bed, I silently got up from my chair. With warm tears rolling profusely down my cheeks, I quietly headed for my bedroom where I poured my feelings of injustice into my pillow for being forgotten and especially for being left alone in the dark!

Stubborn? Yes! Obedient? Oh yes! I did what my father told me to do: I stayed in the dining room until he excused me from the table. But I didn't eat my carrots!

CIVILIAN CONSERVATION CORPS

The Civilian Conservation Corps, more commonly referred to by its acronym (CCC), was established in 1933. This program was placed into action by the newly elected president of the United States, Franklin Delano Roosevelt. Because of the economic depression during 1929, he created a work program for the many unemployed men. At Koke'e there is a small museum, dining room, and curio shop, a stopover for the many tourists passing through today. This is the original site of the ranger station where the men working on CCC projects were housed.

In 1934, Kaua'i saw its first group of CCC workers at Koke'e. I was five years old when I watched the work crew making its trails, but I never knew where they went. In fact, a few trails went nowhere; they simply ended at some point where the next step would be a thousand-foot drop into Waimea Canyon, often called the "Grand Canyon of the Pacific."

One of those trails, called Kumuwela, was built in Halemanu Valley. Although Hurricane Iniki destroyed the original trail to Kumuwela Lookout on September 11, 1992, Kumuwela has retained its spectacular view of Waimea Canyon. Many people do not know where this viewpoint is located simply because no tour bus can get into Halemanu Valley.

Kumuwela Lookout. Below the peak in the upper right-hand corner is where buses stop for tourists to view Waimea Canyon. To the left is one of many trails that went nowhere!

IT WAS LOVE AT FIRST SIGHT!

I was in love; there was no doubt about it. Janet Lee, at only five feet four, was the most beautiful woman I had ever met. Her voice, soft and melodious, had a penetrating quality that demanded attention. When she looked at me, I could feel her love penetrating my inner soul. I knew she was fond of me, but we never voiced these thoughts because there were always too many people around us. Spellbound when her dark brown eyes stared at me, I tried to project thoughts of a deep and sincere love through my eyes.

Janet's dark, silky, shoulder-length hair was often clasped at the back of her neck with a jeweled barrette. I preferred to see her hair long and freely flowing without the clasp. I brazenly tapped her on the shoulder one morning, and when she turned to face me, I courageously asked, "Miss Lee, why do you wear that clasp? Your hair looks pretty without it." She laughed softly and replied, "I wear it to keep my hair from falling over my eyes when I work at my desk." Her response did make sense, of course, but I still liked to see her hair whirl whenever she turned her head.

When Janet Lee walked down the aisle or across the room, all eyes were riveted to her movements. Her dress, swaying side to side, gave the appearance of a woman on a stage modeling dresses. Whatever she wore seemed to mold itself into every curve of her body. I knew the girls were envious, and I think the guys were jealous because I often asked questions about work assignments, usually just so I could be near her.

Not only was she beautiful but she was also very intelligent, knowledgeable in analyzing people, judging them for who they were, understanding their needs, and recognizing their potential qualities. Because she was, in a sense, a group leader, Janet was in a position to request that I be transferred to an advanced level where my work would be better suited to the challenges needed to stimulate my mind. This change, she theorized, would give me a better foundation with greater opportunity to prepare for advancement into a position of leadership.

Although we knew each other less than four months, I felt we were coming to an understanding that if given enough time a budding love could blossom. I was, of course, very disappointed to learn my transfer had been approved and would be effective immediately following New Year's Day.

After a few days at my new location, I knew being in the same work area with Janet Lee would never again be possible. I could only fleetingly say hi as we passed each other in the hallways or whenever we met in the lunchroom.

Many years have gone by since meeting this marvelous creature, who shared her life with everyone around her, gladly giving her time and energy to help others. As I reflect on those moments of pleasure, I remember how devastated I was to learn Janet Lee got married the following summer and would no longer be a first grade teacher at our school.

THE TELEPHONE CALL

· · · · · · · · ● ● ● ● ● ● · · · · · ·

I was six years old, and on a Saturday, this meant no school for two whole days. Neighbors were not really close, generally about a quarter of a mile from each other, but boys did manage to get together on weekends, sometimes at a birthday party, at a picnic on the beach, horseback riding near our mountain cabin, or just hanging around at somebody's house.

One day, at my house, three of us were trying to think of a game we could play. Because we needed four people, we decided to call a playmate just down the road. Taking the telephone receiver off the wall, I spun the crank, one long, two short. There was no answer. Once again, one long, two short, and still no answer. We came to the obvious conclusion that no one was home. Living not too far from our first chum was another who often joined us whenever his mother would let him out of the house. Again I cranked the phone, this time with two long, three short. After two attempts, Basil Hansen's mother answered to tell us Basil was out with his father. Who else could we call? Would it be four short cranks? Two short, one long? Or maybe we could call three short-one long or three long-one short, or two long-two short. It's not hard to guess that trying to remember the number of telephone cranks, long or short, could be very confusing to a six-year-old, so it shouldn't be too surprising that we frequently got the wrong number.

The solution then was to make one short crank and wait for the operator to say, "Billy Wright, who do you kids want this time?" As you can guess, the telephone system was antiquated; everyone was on a "party line," but in a small plantation town in the mid-1930s, this was the most modern equipment available to its residents. The telephone operator was perhaps the only person on the island who recognized the short cranks, the long cranks, and the many combinations the system used. She also knew who was calling who at any given time but kept mum on all the hanky-panky on Kaua'i.

PORTUGUESE SWEET BREAD

Across from the Kekaha Sugar Mill there was a Portuguese community, and at the entrance to the compound stood a huge, round brick oven. This is where community members did a lot of baking, including making Portuguese sweet bread.

While visiting the Lindsay Faye family, two loaves of Portuguese bread were delivered to their house. To this day I can visualize one daughter, Anna, eyeing the warm, fresh sweet bread sitting on the kitchen counter just waiting to be eaten. There was no hesitation when Anna took a carving knife and sliced one end of the loaf to expose the warm bread. Leaving the outer crust intact, she and I cautiously peeled out the bread and ravishingly devoured the "good" part. When we finished eating the bread, Anna carefully replaced the outer crust and rewrapped the package so it looked like a whole loaf. I never did find out what happened when the kitchen maid sliced the empty shell!

THE CIRCUS PERFORMER

· · · · · · ●●●● ● ●● · · · · · ·

The year was 1937. I was eight years old; school was out for the summer. The circus with its Ferris wheel, merry-go-round, cotton candy, ring toss, dart throwing at balloons to win prizes, nickel-and-dime games, sideshows, and whatever oddities were to be seen had come to Hawai'i, to the island of Kaua'i, where I lived. This was the island's annual two-day carnival spree. I loved riding the merry-go-round but was a bit of a fraidy-cat when the Ferris wheel stopped high in the air. I liked the cotton candy, throwing darts at balloons, and all the other wonders of a circus where kids could enjoy an evening of fun and excitement. The crack of a whip as the lions and tigers did their balancing acts on huge balls or jumped from one tabletop to another was really exciting. I laughed when the clowns did their acts.

Perhaps most memorable of all was a show in a separate tent off to one side of the carnival grounds, a tent set well away from the main entrance.

My friend Tony, who was three years younger than me and always curious to see what was going on, grabbed my hand and said, "Let's go to that tent; I want to see what's over there!" Being small had its blessings. We were able to scuffle our way to the small platform where the barker was calling his show a first of its kind in Hawai'i.

The show, I recall, was rather expensive. It cost fifty cents to get in. Leaning toward us, the barker asked in a reprimanding voice, "Your mother know you kids are here?"

"Oh yes," replied Tony. "She said it was okay to come here!"

With skepticism the barker said, "Well, okay. You kids got fifty cents?"

"Oh yes!" Tony responded. Palming my fifty cents, along with his, Tony started to hand it to the barker.

Pointing to a small booth located at the tent entrance, the barker said, "You kids give your money to the man over there!"

Seats were filling up fast and once again, because we were small, we managed to squeeze onto a bench up front near the stage. Actors came on, made some funny remarks that didn't make sense, and then performed some skits that still didn't make any sense. The audience, however, seemed to understand the jokes and laughed raucously.

It was time for the main show. The barker came on stage, again emphasizing a feature never before seen in Hawai'i, and as he started moving off stage, the tent was engulfed in darkness. A soft blue spotlight lit the stage to the left, and there, stepping into the round circle of light, was a very beautiful lady. Except for the music, all was quiet. The dancer moved back and forth from one end of the stage to the other, the spotlight following her to wherever she moved. From the audience there was no laughter, just hushed remarks about how beautiful she was. Whispers mingled with sighs of delight could be heard as the performer did her utmost to entertain the enraptured audience. What fascinated me then and still does to this day is how the two fans she held were so artistically used to show everything, yet show nothing. As you can guess, even an eight-year-old can enjoy an exciting, fascinating, exotic, erotic work of art! I don't really know if it was she, but a few people mentioned the name Sally Rand. I never did tell my mother that Tony and I saw a naked lady do a dance with two huge feathered fans!

WAR GAMES

• • • • • • • • • ● • • • • • • • • •

As a seven-year-old living in the small community of Kekaha on the island of Kaua'i in the 1930s, finding boys of the same age to play with did present a problem, especially when the nearest neighbor was a quarter of a mile or so away. However, boys will be boys, and on Saturdays we managed to find each other. A favorite game was War! Each team would consist of two or three boys. The place to play this game was at the Kekaha Sugar Plantation stables where mules and horses were resting after a hard week of labor in the sugarcane fields. We would rake dried manure into embankments that served as forts, and once that was accomplished, we would lob missiles at each other, occasionally running outside the protective barrier to outflank the "enemy." Ammunition was plentiful. There was the soft puffy stuff that would spread over the enemy like talcum powder. Then there was the fresh, mushy, smelly ammo, the type just recently recycled by the horses and mules—you know, the nasty stuff! Because fresh ammo was so nasty, we didn't use it often, but we did use it.

Having learned my lesson about how nasty those fresh missiles could be, I often took a pot from my house to use as a helmet before marching off to war. In one battle, after yelling, "Time out," I removed the pot to brush the gooey stuff off my helmet and immediately got zapped with a direct hit on my head. I was so angry

I picked up whatever ammo I could find and started throwing it toward the enemy. That was a big mistake! This made me a target for everyone, even those on my side. Missiles flew in from my right, from my left, in front of me, and even behind me. Everyone was bombarding me. To this day, I don't remember hitting anyone during my defensive maneuver. This just wasn't my day.

With the odor of manure covering me from head to toe, I was attacked on my way home by f lies - in my hair, ears, nose, and everywhere. When I got home, my mother must have seen me heading for the front door but stopped me just as I was taking the first step onto the porch of our house. She took one look at me with all that manure on my clothes and promptly told me to get a lawn hose and take a bath outside, clothes and all. "And when you finish," she added, "take my pot and scrub it!" To this day I'm still wondering if it was a stifled laugh I saw on my mother's face when she quickly spun around to go back into the house.

A BRIGHT SUNDAY MORNING

Pausing on a step just past Kamehameha and Liholiho dormitories, leading toward the Kamehameha School for Boys cafeteria, a light breeze brushed the cool, damp air down the back of my neck and into my shirt. As the early morning sunrise crept slowly over the mountain crest, the chill in the air started to subside. To the northeast, the white clouds silently drifting westward toward the ocean were constantly changing from one form into another. I visualized an elephant transforming into the shape of a man smoking a pipe. "That's great," I said to myself, "the old man looks good smoking a pipe." As if in a magical world, a small puff of black smoke appeared at the bowl of his pipe followed by a second, and then a third. Toward the west was the calm ocean, its gentle waves lazily moving toward the shoreline. Except for the waves stretching into a long, thin line, one following another, the water surface looked like a smooth sheet of glass. As the sun rose higher, the morning chill drifted away.

Down the hillside, houses became clearer and brighter, gradually becoming a part of the quiet city that stretched below. Sunlight touching the valley between the Wai'ainae Mountain Range and the Ko'olau Mountains off to my right brought forth shades of green with patches of brown scattered on its slopes. As the air around me started to feel warmer, I moved under the overhanging eave of the assembly hall at the bottom of the stairs that led to the classrooms and dining hall.

Bees buzzed in and out of the flowered pathway; birds in a nearby tree were noisily chirping their early morning greetings to each other, welcoming another new day. And as more clouds drifted by, shaped in a fantasy of imagined objects, the peacefulness of another wonderful day surrounded me. This was the type of day I could spend reading a book in my room. Oh well, it didn't matter; it was almost eight o'clock and time for breakfast. Some of the students were already strolling toward the mess hall; I joined them. Turning to Norwin Jones, a classmate and cousin who was walking beside me, I said, "Hey, Jones, look at that puffy cloud."

"Yeah," he replied, "kinda goofy, looks like a black cotton ball. Look, Willie, there's another one."

This was Sunday morning, December 7, 1941.

Approximately 240 cadets were enrolled at Kamehameha School for Boys, a school based on ROTC military training. The cadets, in seventh through twelfth grade, occupied six dormitories. It wasn't long before groups of ten to fifteen students clustered throughout the campus were wondering what was happening. Meanwhile, in the dining room, a cadet officer entered and yelled, "Return to your dormitories!"

Back in my dormitory, Lunalilo Hall, someone had a radio tuned to KGU, one of two radio stations on O'ahu. The announcer had been repeating, "This is the real McCoy. Japanese planes are attacking Pearl Harbor and Hickam Field. Get under cover! All military personnel report to your stations immediately!"

As students disappeared into their dormitories, a few climbed through the window of their room onto the overhanging eaves facing Pearl Harbor and Hickam Field. I joined them. The sky was dense with puffs of black smoke from antiaircraft guns. To the right, off in the distance, antiaircraft shells hit an airplane; spiraling smoke marked the trail of the aircraft before it exploded in a sugarcane field that was part of the Waipahu Sugar Plantation. Within a few minutes, a huge column of black smoke moved skyward. The battleship USS *Arizona*, the pride of the United States Navy, was taking its final breath for survival. Suddenly, a second belch of black smoke arose from Pearl Harbor. Several months later I learned the second column of smoke came from a direct hit into the forward powder magazine of a destroyer, the USS *Shaw*, tearing the entire bow off the ship. Torpedo attacks on the USS *Oklahoma* caused that huge battleship to capsize on its port side in the shallow harbor.

Three airplanes in a tight V-formation f lew over the school campus, the deafening roar of their engines drowning all

Zero Fighter

conversation. So close were the aircraft we could see the rising sun painted under the wings of the planes and the tiny faces of

the pilots inside the cockpit. Still wondering what was happening, some of us waved to the pilots, and in recognition, one pilot nodded as if returning a salute to those who waved. Several hours later, when we realized we were witnessing a war between the United States and Japan, we guessed these three aircraft had come from their primary target, Kane'ohe Naval Air Station, and were now headed toward their secondary target, Pearl Harbor.

An antiaircraft shell exploded less than 150 yards to our left along the rock wall of the road leading to the girl's campus, near the access road to the six dormitories. The explosive force and the loud boom startled and scared us. Then, and only then, did we realize the enormity of what the radio announcer was saying: "Get under cover!" In response to the loud blast, cadet officers and teachers ordered us back inside the dormitory. Dutifully heeding their commands, we crawled back through the windows and inside to safety. As lower classmen, we did what cadet officers told us to do. We entered our rooms; removed sheets, blankets, pillow, and mattress; and carried them to the middle floor of our three-story dormitory, placing our bedding along the hallway walls. This was the safest location in case enemy planes strafed our dormitory. I placed my bedding near the lavatory, not because it was in the middle of the hallway and the safest location but more so because that was the only space left in the hallway. With two floors of bedding being placed on one floor, the hallway was getting crowded. My third-floor room was located on the mauka, or Diamond Head, side of Lunalilo Hall. My curiosity was still aroused; I wanted to see what was happening outside. Entering one of the rooms facing Hickam Field and Pearl Harbor, I noticed someone else had the same idea. He, too, was curious. One … two … three dust clouds were rising in front of the hangars at Hickam Field!

"Wow," I said to him, "those bombs missed the hangars!" Several years later movies were released to the public showing that the Japanese bombs were right on target; American aircraft were parked in front of the hangars, not inside the building.

Bordering one end of Hickam Field was a narrow inlet used by navy ships to enter or leave Pearl Harbor. Steaming straight and as fast as it could go through the inlet was a white ship, black smoke belching from its funnels. A spray of white water leaped high astern of the vessel followed by a long trail of white churning water created by its propellers. Once clear of the harbor buoys, the ship started a zigzag maneuver to avoid the bombs being dropped around it.

In 1954, as an engineering aide at Westinghouse Aerospace Division in Baltimore, I read a naval report about hull damage on the warships exposed to the bombing attack on December 7, 1941. Not until then did I realize that the destroyer, the USS *Helm*, was the same vessel I watched leaving Pearl Harbor that fateful morning. In October 1998, while attending a meeting at a private residence in San Diego, another story about the USS *Helm* arose. The captain was scheduled to leave Pearl Harbor on a one-day trip around O'ahu. On board was the captain's nine-year-old son. When the first wave of attackers reached Pearl Harbor around 0800, the USS *Helm* was already underway passing Ford Island, the navy's airfield inside the harbor. When the attack took place, the *Helm*, at flank speed, made a beeline to get out of the narrow channel. That's when I saw the churning white water at the stern of the vessel and the heavy black smoke from the ship's funnel.

There was another report on the sinking of a midget submarine that managed to get into Pearl Harbor by following a tugboat that had been towing a target raft used for gunnery practice at sea. When the attack on Pearl Harbor started, the USS *Monaghan* left its mooring at the north end of the harbor, and while steaming toward the narrow inlet, it ran over the submarine and dropped depth charges, but in the shallow water the *Monaghan's* propeller shaft was damaged. Only after repairs were completed a few days later did the USS *Monaghan* proceed out into the vast Pacific Ocean searching for the Japanese fleet.

During the attack, students with cameras took pictures of whatever came into view. Teachers, with the help of cadet officers, were ordered to confiscate all cameras, a reason not readily apparent to us at that time. Several months later, a family friend assigned to naval intelligence gave me a reason.

"From your school," he said, "you can see Hickam Field and Pearl Harbor pretty well, and camera film, small though it might be, could be enlarged to show the massive destruction the attack had on our military installations. If the film got into enemy hands," he added, "they could assess how much damage was done, and how ill prepared our military forces were, and launch an invasion force against us."

For ROTC classes in marksmanship, .22 caliber rifles were issued, but for daily exercises and parades, cadets used .30-caliber Model 1903 bolt-action Springfield rifles. Within two hours of the attack, army trucks were at our school picking up rifles and ammunition from the school armory. Cadets who were eighteen years old were immediately conscripted into the army. As ROTC cadets at Kamehameha, these students were already considered to have had basic infantry training. In less than two hours of the Japanese attack, boys became men. Cadet officers not yet eighteen years old were given the responsibility of protecting a water tower located a half mile above the school campus. Ten cadets, most of them juniors and seniors, were selected to hike up the mountainside to the tower. Senior cadets who were officers wore their sabers. This was the only weapon they carried. It was fortunate they did not have a portable radio to hear rumors that Japanese paratroopers were poisoning the water supply.

Although no paratroopers landed on O'ahu, the rumors gave us some anxious moments. As the morning sunlight filtered through the trees, half of the "men" returned from the water tower to get something to eat. No one had slept so their eyes were bloodshot, they were cold and hungry, and their khaki uniforms were muddied from hiking up the wet mountain slope. All looked like frightened rabbits. These were sixteen- and seventeen-year-old "soldiers" thrown into a war of which we knew little or nothing.

A constant stream of ambulances from the navy hospital near Pearl Harbor transferred military wives with their newborn babies to the infirmary at the Kamehameha School for Boys. (See article printed in the school newspaper, *Ka Moi*, on January 23, 1942.)

Around nine o'clock that night, with a total blackout in effect, machine guns with tracer bullets could be seen and heard over Pearl Harbor. Airplanes from the USS *Enterprise* attempting to land on Ford Island were mistaken as another Japanese attack. They were shot down before being identified as friendly. Only a few pilots from the *Enterprise* survived this ordeal.

Two days after the attack, by order of the military and school authorities, parents were told to pick up their children and take them home. It took three days to complete this task. Thirty-four students from outer islands who had no family on O'ahu and couldn't get back to their homes were asked to remain at Kamehameha School as campus guards.

Because martial law had been declared, soldiers were instructed to shoot anyone seen on the streets one-half hour after sunset and one hour before sunrise. Martial law dictated a total blackout creating an ominous and eerie feeling. For three weeks my parents, my sister, and I stayed with friends who lived inland on St. Louis Heights away from the shoreline.

PEARL HARBOR: AFTERMATH

· · · · · · · ●● ●● ●● · · · · ·

On Sunday, December 7, 1941, the Japanese launched a surprise attack against the United States military. By planning the attack on a Sunday morning, Admiral Nagumo, under the command of Admiral Isoroku Yamamoto, hoped to catch the entire Pacific fleet, including our aircraft carriers, in port. As luck would have it, the three United States carriers assigned to the Pacific area were not in Pearl Harbor. The USS *Enterprise* was returning from Wake Island where it had just delivered aircraft to that base, the USS *Lexington* was ferrying aircraft to Midway Island, and the USS *Saratoga* and one battleship, USS *Colorado*, were at West Coast ports undergoing repairs.

In spite of the latest intelligence reports about the missing aircraft carriers (his most important targets), Admiral Nagumo decided to continue the attack and launched 423 aircraft from his six aircraft carriers. A three-wave attack was planned. At 0600 hours, at a range of 230 miles north of O'ahu, Admiral Nagumo launched his first wave of forty Nakajima B5N2 "Kate" torpedo bombers, thirty Aichi D3A1 "Val" dive-bombers, fifty high-altitude bombers, and forty-three "Zeros," which struck their targets at 0753 hours. Prior to the first strike, the Japanese envoys in Washington, DC, were expected to deliver Japan's ultimatum declaring war on the United States. Because the attack took place *before* this declaration, the term "sneak attack" became a rallying cry for Americans.

The second wave, launched at 0715 hours, reached its objectives an hour after the first strike. The first wave of attackers struck the airfields (Hickam, Wheeler, Ewa, and Kane'ohe) and the fleet anchored in Pearl Harbor. The second wave of 167 fighter aircraft and thirty-seven dive-bombers continued their attack on the same targets. The third wave of attackers would destroy the navy's fuel tanks sitting on a hillside, in plain view, overlooking Pearl Harbor. Honolulu's power plant, located at the north end of Pearl Harbor in Pearl City, Waimalu area, would have been destroyed with the third wave of attackers. However, not knowing where our aircraft carriers were and, thus, possibly leaving his force exposed to a counterattack, Admiral Nagumo canceled the third strike and headed home.

At Kamehameha our Sunday meal started at 0800, just about the time the first wave of Japanese aircraft struck Pearl Harbor. The dining room windows facing the harbor gave us an unobstructed view of what was occurring during the raid. Tom Mountain, one of the instructors at Kamehameha, returned to his table where seven cadets were seated. He remarked, "Boy, today's maneuvers are the most realistic I've ever seen!" My cousin Norwin Jones, an eighth grader, was one of the cadets at that table.

Around 8:30 a.m., as we finished our meal, a cadet officer burst into the dining room and yelled, "Everybody out! Report back to your dormitory, *now!*" It was during the second wave of the attack, while sitting outside our dormitory window, that we saw the three airplanes f lying over our school on their way to Pearl Harbor.

When the attacks ended, American losses were as follows:

Casualties:	Army	Navy	Marines	Civilians
KIA	233	1,998	109	48
WIA	364	710	69	225

Battleships:

USS *Arizona*—total loss when a bomb hit her powder magazine

USS *Oklahoma*—total loss when she capsized and sank

USS *California*—sunk, later raised and repaired

USS *West Virginia*—sunk, later raised and repaired

USS *Nevada*—underway but beached to prevent blocking the channel

USS *Pennsylvania*—light damage USS *Maryland*—light damage

USS *Tennessee*—light damage

USS *Utah*—former battleship used as a target, sunk

Cruisers:

USS *New Orleans*—light damage USS *San Francisco*—light damage USS *Detroit*—light damage

USS *Raleigh*—heavily damaged but repaired

USS *Helena*—light damage

USS *Honolulu*—light damage

Destroyers:

USS *Downes*—destroyed, parts salvaged USS *Cassin*—destroyed, parts salvaged USS *Shaw*—major damage

USS *Helm*—light damage

USS *Monaghan*—propeller damaged while depth charging a m id g et submarine inside Pearl Harbor

USS *Oglala* (minelayer)—sunk but later raised and repaired

USS *Curtiss* (seaplane tender)—severely damaged but later repaired
USS *Vestal* (repair ship)—severely damaged but later repaired
USS *Sotoyomo* (harbor tug)—sunk but later raised and repaired

The submarine base was virtually left untouched and intact as a unit.

Japanese Ships in Hawaii, December 7, 1941

Aircraft Carriers	Sunk at	
Kaga	Midway	June 4. 1942
Soryu	Midway	June 4, 1942
Hiryu	Midway	June 5, 1942
Akagi	Midway	June 5, 1942
Shokaku	Philippine Sea	June 19, 1944
Zuikaku	Leyte Gulf	Oct. 25, 1944

Battleships	Sunk at	
Hei	Guadalcanal	Nov. 13, 1943
Kirishima	Guadalcanal	Nov. 14, 1943

Heavy Cruisers	Sunk at	
Chikuma	Leyte Gulf	Oct. 25, 1944
Tome	Kure	July 24, 1945

Light Cruisers	Sunk at	
Katori	Truk	Feb. 17, 1944
Abukuma	Suriagao Strait	Oct. 27, 1944

Destroyers	Sunk at	
Arare	Aleutians	July 5, 1942
Kagero	Solomons	May 8, 1943
Suzanami	Yap	June 14, 1944
Akigumo	Celebes Sea	April 11, 1944
Tanikaze	Tawi Tawi	June 9, 1944

Shiranuhi	Leyte Gulf	Oct. 27, 1944
Urakaze	Formosa	Nov. 21, 1944
Hamakaze	South of Kyushu	April 7, 1945
Isokaze	South of Kyushu	April 7, 1945
Kazumi	South of Kyushu	April 7, 1945
Ushio	Surrender at Yokosuka	July 18, 1945

Submarines

Thirty submarines and four two-man midget submarines were sunk. One two–man sub, beached on O'ahu on December 8, 1941, was placed in front of Honolulu City Hall for several months and exploited for war bond purchases.

Undamaged from the attack, the cruiser USS *Phoenix* sailed past the USS *Arizona* en route to the open sea to seek out the enemy.

In June 2009, sixty-eight and a half years after the attack on Pearl Harbor, a Kodak Brownie camera was discovered in a footlocker; you may have to go to a museum to see what a Brownie camera looks like. The film was developed and distributed via Internet. The sailor who took these pictures was a crew member on the USS *Quapaw*.

Realizing when the camera was discovered and when the pictures were taken and developed, it is incredible and remarkable to see the quality of the reproductions. Here are some of the photographs retrieved through the Internet.

29

31

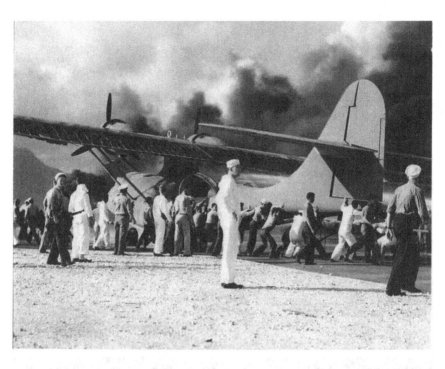

This photograph appears to be a close-up of the picture shown above. Note the similarity of the crow's nest in the two photos.

The submarine base was virtually left untouched during the attack.
All vessels were stocked, fueled, and ready for sea duty within two days.

Waikiki Beach in early 1942.
All barbed wire was removed from beaches in late 1943

Four million feet of barbed wire was posted on O'ahu beaches.

The Matson Navigation Company built the Royal Hawaiian Hotel (in the background) in 1927 as an icon of luxury for passengers traveling to Honolulu or on their way to Australia. It was reserved exclusively for submarine crews during World War II.

KAHUNA OF DEATH

• • • • • • ● ● ● ● • • • • • •

One morning during the summer of 1944, my sister, Carolyn, as a normal routine started to roll out of her bed, but when she attempted to stand, she was struck with violent pain. She was unable to put any weight on her right foot. She also had an earache and a stiff neck. Because of these multiple ailments, my mother called our family physician, who came to see my sister at our house.

While she was on the bed, the doctor made his examination and, upon completing his investigation, declared he could find no physical evidence of injury anywhere. This, of course, was puzzling because every time the doctor asked my sister to do something he had to repeat his request. She had difficulty hearing what he was asking her to do. The worst condition was not being able put any weight on her foot. The doctor suggested my mother take my sister to the hospital where routine tests could be made to determine the cause of the pain. Because she was hurting so much, my sister refused to get out of bed.

Jane Thurston, my mother's sister who lived next door to us, suggested contacting a *kahuna*, a Hawaiian healer, to see my sister. My mother consented. The next day the kahuna visited us, and immediately upon entering the bedroom where my sister lay, she said, "Oh my, I feel an evil spirit is in this room!" The kahuna made a visual inspection and proceeded to physically massage my sister's right foot, ankle, and calf, as well as her neck. After about five minutes of massaging, the kahuna made a startling remark. She declared my sister had been placed under the spell of another kahuna, a kahuna of *death*! The story she told was incredible. I was in that room and heard it in its entirety. She said there was a family member who was causing this condition; the kahuna could not name the individual involved.

While the kahuna was massaging my sister's body, she would excitedly declare, "Look, look, there is a spirit leaving this girl; there's another one!"

After questioning my sister about her activities, it was determined that she had spent the previous weekend visiting the daughter of my mother's cousin. When my sister came home, she had left a sock, an earring, and a shell necklace at that house. These were the items used to place a spell on my sister.

None of us in the room saw anything, but shortly after the kahuna left our house, my sister fell asleep. Several hours later she got out of bed and went to the bathroom. She felt no pain when standing, no earache, and no stiff neck.

A few days after this incident my mother and her sister went to Kaimuki where their relative lived and confronted her with this incredible story. Denying any activity regarding the kahuna of death, my mother and aunt retrieved the sock, the earring, and the shell necklace my sister had left at that house. It was assumed jealousy was the motive. My sister was popular and easily mingled among other teenagers; her daughter was not sociable and didn't get along with other girls.

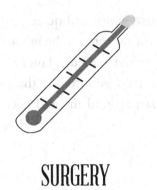

SURGERY

· · · · · · ●●● ● ●●● · · · · ·

Two teenagers from McKinley High School in Honolulu aspiring to be future nurses were assigned as hospital trainees at Queen's Hospital. A nurse who was explaining the rudiments of this profession accompanied the two girls. Pausing at the foot of my bed, the nurse handed them my bedside chart and said, "I want you girls to do the preliminary preparations tomorrow morning before Mr. Wright goes into surgery." Their reply was an obedient "Yes, ma'am!"

The next morning, after taking a relaxant prior to surgery, I noticed the young ladies shyly walking toward my bed. Picking up the chart, glancing at me, and then looking back at the chart, one whispered to the other, "You do it!" In an equally quiet tone, almost inaudible, the second girl said, "No, you do it!" Although I was a bit sleepy, I detected what I thought were giggles from each of the young ladies. Because they didn't want to awaken me, they replaced the chart and promptly walked out of the room.

Around ten thirty that morning I was wheeled into the surgery room where I was gently and efficiently lifted from the gurney onto the operating table where the anesthesiologist, two nurses, the doctor performing the operation, and an intern/observer were waiting. Lifting the sheet to expose my legs and abdomen, the surgeon angrily remarked, "Why wasn't this patient prepared for surgery before he was brought here?"

I could see one nurse wince and quietly say to the other, "Damn those aides, I thought they wanted to be nurses!"

As a seventeen-year-old patient (January 1946), I guess it was just too much for the teenagers to lift the sheet, expose my nude body, and shave the hair around my abdomen in preparation for an appendectomy.

WHAT'S A HOT DOG?

I always thought a hot dog with relish, mustard and ketchup was a great snack while watching a football or baseball game. When I was eighteen, I discovered another definition for *hot dog*. Upon arriving in San Francisco in August 1947, I submitted my application to San Jose Junior College (now known as San Jose State University) and the University of San Francisco. Both schools accepted my application, which gave me a chance to select the one I wanted. My choice was USF simply because a fifty-mile train ride from Mountain View to San Francisco was more appealing than a forty-five-minute bus ride to San Jose.

A major curriculum at USF was the Reserve Officers' Training Corps (ROTC) program. The uniforms issued were styled for all army officers, very chic and certainly appealing to the opposite sex.

Thanksgiving weekend was a long break from studies, and on a whim my cousin, with whom I shared a room in Mountain View, suggested we take a flight to Los Angeles to visit his sister. She lived on Beverly Boulevard about a half block south of the corner of Beverly and Western Avenues.

At Beverly and Western there was a small three-story hotel that had a bar on the ground floor. After checking into the hotel, he suggested I wear the ROTC uniform so the bartender wouldn't question my age. The drinking age in California was twenty-one. While sitting at the bar, my cousin attempted to get the interest of a female customer. Unfortunately, he had a slight problem; she wasn't interested in his advances and kept me in their conversation. Perhaps it was the military officer's uniform or possibly because I wasn't showing any interest, or maybe it was my baby-faced expression that attracted her attention. Earlier during this episode, my cousin explained that if he was successful with his advances, I would have to find another place for the night. I readily understood the gist of that statement, and as far as I was concerned, that was fine with me. However, the girl whom he was attempting to capture kept moving away from him and hanging on to me. I was definitely naive and tried to find a reason why she seemed attracted to me. I never did figure that one out and didn't really care.

It was obvious to my cousin he wasn't getting anywhere close to achieving his goal, so he motioned me toward the men's room. He told me if I needed the hotel room that was fine with him. I really wasn't interested in pursuing this adventure because it never had been my intention to do anything about the situation. I was only eighteen and didn't realize this was often referred to as "living it up," a fact of life!

Upon returning to our seats at the bar, the woman asked if I would take her home. Being the gentleman I thought I was, I readily agreed.

Hailing a taxi outside the hotel, I followed my companion into the backseat. What sounded like a casual afterthought, she said, "I'm hungry; I want a hot dog!"

Turning to the driver, I asked him if he knew of any hot-dog stands still open at such a late hour. It was one o'clock in the morning.

Looking directly into my face, he said, "Is that what you want?" I promptly replied, "Yes!"

As we drove around the area looking for a hot-dog stand, my companion sidled up to me and started to rub my knees while taking my left hand and placing it under her dress on the inside of her right leg. Her actions actually made me nervous and uncomfortable.

Fifteen minutes later, the cab driver pulled over to the curb, turned to me, and said, "Mister, I don't think we're going to find any hot-dog stand open at this hour!" He had a Cheshire-like grin on his face.

Because it was apparent my companion wasn't getting anywhere with her advances, she said to me, "Why don't you take me home. I live just a few blocks from here." She gave the address to the driver and off we went. Upon reaching our destination, I stepped out of the cab, told the cab driver to wait for me, and escorted my companion to her front door. When she entered her house, I left.

Upon entering the cab, the driver, with a huge grin on his face, asked, "Mister, do you know what she wanted?"

I replied, "Yeah, she was hungry and wanted a hot dog!"

With that statement, the cab driver just shook his head and drove me back to my hotel.

AT-11, THE ADVENTURE I MISSED

• • • • • • • • ● • • • • • • • •

The year was 1947; World War II had ended two years earlier. The United Nations Relief and Rehabilitation Administration (UNRRA) had been organized to help the war-torn world by sending surplus war material to our allies. In Honolulu, the AT-11, a round- bottomed, wooden-hulled, oceangoing US Army tug, was being readied to take a river-dredging barge with its derrick and crane to China. Its destination was Shanghai, where the harbor on the Yangtze River would be dredged to accommodate vessels requiring deeper water. Upon arriving in Shanghai, our captain was instructed to sign everything over to the government of Nationalist China, then under the leadership of Generalissimo Chiang Kai-shek.

UNRRA had an advertisement in the Honolulu *Advertiser*, a local newspaper; it was hiring people to take equipment to China. No experience was required, but you had to be at least eighteen years of age and hold a seaman's registration document from the US Coast Guard.

China! Shanghai! Yangtze River! This was exciting! This was intriguing! Except for the Coast Guard registration, I had all the major qualifications for the job: eighteen years old and no experience. Upon receiving my Z-number certification from the Coast Guard office in Honolulu, I signed on as a "food handler," another term for "messman." Because of my late arrival as a crew member, I was instructed to report to the US Public Health Service a few blocks from the pier for inoculations. No one told me I had to take nine shots covering typhoid, diphtheria, cholera, tetanus, yellow fever, whooping cough, smallpox, chickenpox, and measles in one day at one sitting. After taking four shots in one arm, the doctor asked if my arm hurt. I remarked that it did, so he said, "Let's finish the job by balancing the weight to the other arm." He was smiling, of course, and really seemed to enjoy my agony. When he said, "Well, that's the last one," that's when I fainted!

With the nurse bent over me gently tapping my face and asking if I was all right, and the doctor standing behind her with a big grin on his face, I felt a bit foolish. In a low tone with a smirk still on his face, he said, "I guess I shouldn't have told you that was your last shot for today. If you're okay, you can report back to your ship and by the way," he continued, "here are your papers authorizing the clinic on Johnson Island to give you booster shots for the ones I gave you today. You'll get your third booster shots for tetanus, diphtheria, typhoid, and cholera when you get to Guam. You won't be in another American port so all your immunizations have to be completed by the time your ship leaves that island," he added.

"Holy mackerel," I cussed to myself, "I have to take more of this?"

Three days later, on Wednesday, June 2, the crew was told to be on board by 0600. We were cleared to enter Pearl Harbor to pick up the derrick and crane. Although I had been a member of the crew only a week, and because the ship was tied to a pier in Honolulu, I spent my nights at home.

At 0530 on June 2, with exuberance and anticipation that this day would be the beginning of an exciting adventure, I arrived at the pier to board our ship only to be met by a forlorn crew. The third engineer had fallen asleep on his watch, causing the boilers to burn out. We weren't going anywhere. What a disappointment! We now had to wait for a tugboat to tow our tugboat into Pearl Harbor for repairs. For another four weeks we remained on board as paid crewmen until one day the skipper called us together and said we would sign off but would be called back when repairs were completed and the ship was readied for the journey. "A dry dock in Pearl Harbor won't be ready for us until September," he told us.

With that information, I decided to take my first trip to the West Coast as a passenger on the SS *Matsonia,* one of two Matson Company ships that had resumed their San Francisco-Hawai'i-Los Angeles passenger service following the end of World War II. A week after arriving in San Francisco, I received a letter from my father advising me that I had received a letter from UNRRA asking crew members to report back to the AT-11. "A dry-dock facility is available earlier than had been anticipated," he wrote.

Although I didn't take that trip to Shanghai, I did meet a fellow crewman a year later in Seattle who told me the tug left Pearl Harbor on August 4. He told me that with the derrick and crane in tow, the AT-11 made a one-day refueling stop at Johnson Island after ten days at sea. Two and a half weeks after leaving Johnson Island, the AT-11 made a two-day stopover on Guam to get provisions and fuel before continuing on to Shanghai. "Two weeks after we left Guam, we got hit by a typhoon that nearly capsized our ship," he said. "We thought we were going to die!" He told me the barge holding the crane and derrick had sprung a leak and was slowly sinking. "In that typhoon we had no way to board the barge to put a bailing pump on it, even if we had a spare pump." The captain notified the navy and Coast Guard that he was cutting the towline before the derrick and dredging equipment dragged the AT-11 and its crew to a watery grave.

In my case, I'm glad to be relating the episode without being a part of that nightmare.

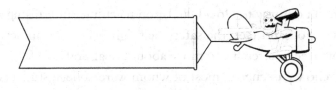

SEATTLE - HONOLULU

• • • • • • • • ● ● ● • • • • • •

Have you ever traveled on a DC-4 propeller-driven aircraft? Fascinating! In August 1948, Northwest Airlines started offering flights between Honolulu and Seattle with a stopover in Portland.

During the Christmas season of 1948, students from colleges and universities in the Seattle area boarded a flight to Honolulu to spend their Christmas and New Year holidays in Hawai'i.

Because of aircraft weight restrictions, everyone was asked his or her weight. To the woman standing ahead of me at the check-in counter, the clerk asked a routine question: "Ma'am, how much do you weigh?"

With an indignant response, she replied, "One hundred forty-five pounds."

"Is this your bag, ma'am?" the clerk asked.

"Yes," she replied.

"I'll have to charge you twenty-one dollars. Passengers are allowed only forty-four pounds of lug gage," he stated.

"That can't be right," she replied. "I weighed it after I packed my clothes. My scale at home said it was at least three pounds under the weight limit!"

My eyes roamed toward the ceiling as I thought, *"Yeah, lady, the scale probably showed your weight at two hundred and thirty pounds without the suitcase."*

Stepping up to the counter, the clerk asked my weight, took my suitcase, read the baggage 'scale, gave me a boarding pass, and said, "Okay, Mr. Wright, have a nice flight!"

The f light left Seattle around 6:00 p.m. with a scheduled stop to pick up more passengers in Portland. At 9:00 p.m. we left Portland

and were on our way to Honolulu. Upon reaching our cruising altitude of twelve thousand feet, the safety belt light went out, indicating we were now free to stretch and move about the aircraft.

My fellow passengers, most of whom were college students happy to be away from their studies, were already in a festive mood. From overhead storage racks, musical instruments appeared, and those who had a guitar or ukulele started strumming and singing familiar Hawaiian tunes. The area having the most room was around the galley at the rear of the aircraft. Not wanting to miss out on the fun, several girls joined the group and started dancing their hula numbers to the beat of our music. The festive mood was short lived when the flight officer, who had been watching us from the sideline, broke in before we started another hula number. "I can see you people are having an early start on Christmas, but would you please spread yourselves along the aisle of the aircraft? The captain is having difficulty trimming the aircraft." With that statement, he illustrated the problem by placing his left arm parallel to the floor of the cabin, tilting his fingers upward while lowering his elbow. We got the point. Apparently the aircraft was flying with its tail dragging. "It's okay if three or four stay in the galley area but, please, no more than four." With that comment he walked back to the pilot's compartment.

Oh well, the hour of midnight, West Coast time, had already passed so we all decided to get some sleep. Upon settling into the comfortable wide seats, the monotonous drone of the four engines and the constant vibration throughout the DC-4 had a lulling effect on us. The fat lady sitting two rows in front of me was snoring just loud enough to blend with the noise of the engines. The f light, I recall, was a pleasant one.

As the morning sunlight filtered throughout the aircraft, a hearty breakfast of ham, scrambled eggs, toast, and coffee was served. Around ten thirty we approached Honolulu airport, Hawaiian time, nearly sixteen hours after leaving Portland, Oregon.

Flight times between Honolulu and Seattle now run approximately five hours. Perhaps in the near future people will be flying between these two points in less than an hour.

PANCAKES

· · · · · · · ●●●● ● ●●● · · · · ·

We all know what a pancake is, especially when it is part of a breakfast menu, perhaps served with a side dish of sausage or ham and eggs, hash brown potatoes, and corn bread with lots of butter. In fact, I'm sure many people really enjoy pancakes made from various types of batter such as blueberry, raspberry, and strawberry. And when those scrumptious pancakes are topped with good maple syrup, coconut syrup, or strawberry or raspberry jam, and served with a hot cup of coffee or tea, or a glass of cold milk, it's a great way to start a new day, especially on a lazy Sunday morning.

During May 1948 the *Agnes Foss*, with its powerful twin diesel engines, had been at sea for twenty-five days, towing two huge barges filled with army surplus material picked up in Honolulu for transfer to the West Coast. It would be at least two days before our first stop: Astoria, a small port town along the Oregon coastline just twelve miles from the mouth of the Columbia River. However, the *Agnes Foss* had a major problem!

"Hey, Cookie, what's for breakfast?"

"Pancakes!" he replied.

"Great! What are we having for lunch?"

"Pancakes!" was the reply.

"Okay, what's for dinner?"

"Pancakes!" Cookie responded.

In less than five seconds, the officers and crew on the *Agnes Foss* became aware of its predicament. Except for pancake batter, the ship's galley was empty. Disaster had struck the crew on the *Agnes Foss*! As an occasional meal, pancakes can be delightful, but when it becomes a matter of survival on a tugboat moving at only four knots per hour and two hundred miles from the nearest land, pancakes served three times a day, two days in a row, can have a devastating effect on any crew in the middle of nowhere.

Although there was no mutiny, it was very much apparent to the captain that there was an immediate problem—in fact, a major problem: morale. Nothing could be done about it, of course, so the crew had to live with a diet of pancakes for breakfast, lunch, and dinner. Since the *Agnes Foss* was carrying a few crates of pineapples for the owner of the Foss Tug and Barge Company, the captain ordered the crates of pineapples opened as a supplement for the meals. One variety of pancake still vivid in my mind is crushed pineapple mixed with the pancake batter. Since that trip, I've had a distinct dislike for pineapple pancakes.

Two days later, waiting at our assigned pier in Astoria were cases and cases of food supplies. These were the first items loaded on board. With orders from the captain, the ship's cook had to give the crew whatever they wanted. My choice was a big, twenty-ounce New York steak cooked medium rare, and although I'm a rice eater, I opted for mashed potatoes and gravy. The rest of the crew made their choices known to the cook. I think one crewman wanted apple pie for his dessert. As for me, I remember having a gigantic chocolate sundae topped with walnuts and maraschino cherries. After two days of pancakes and pineapples, this was truly an unforgettable meal!

Statue of Lion in Twelfth Street Park
Las Vegas, New Mexico

KAPPA THETA

· · · · · · ● · ● · ● · · · ·

Hazing is a tradition at colleges and universities where fraternities and sororities are a part of the school system, and so it was at New Mexico Highlands University (Las Vegas, New Mexico) where I enrolled for the fall quarter of 1949. As a new student from the Territory of Hawai'i (statehood did not occur until 1959), with the thought of wild parties and a sense of brotherhood, friendship, and good fellowship, I joyously accepted an invitation to join a fraternity, Kappa Theta.

Four of us were being pledged that year, but a series of things had to be accomplished before being fully accepted as a fraternity brother. Reflecting on what was required of us in order to become a member of Kappa Theta has made me realize how inane our assignments were.

One task was to look for a pregnant alley cat—at midnight! Have you ever tried to find a cooperative alley cat anytime, anywhere, and especially at night? They make such a hellish ruckus screeching like banshees loud enough to wake the dead! To residents who are trying to get their beauty rest, this is no laughing matter! I had been told that nearly everyone in this town owned a gun of some sort, mostly shotguns or carbine rifles used for hunting coyotes or shooting rattlesnakes when they were on the range rounding up stray cattle—or perhaps prowlers in their backyard? Because we were threading our way through the neighborhood at a late hour, the thought of guns possibly being aimed in our direction was not exactly my idea of an enriching education at New Mexico Highlands University.

On another night we were given two cans of paint, one orange and one black, the colors adopted by the fraternity as its badge of recognition. Our task was to paint a statue located in the middle of the town's public park. The statue was a lion perched on a pedestal in a small triangular park on Twelfth Street across from the Coyote Cafe. I am reminded of the location because quite often I would walk to the cafe to drink coffee and do a bit of studying. The Santa Fe Railroad Depot was located a block or so behind the cafe. There weren't enough trees to hide behind so the task was exceptionally difficult. If we were caught, our fearless foursome would be trapped like rats on a raft in the middle of a frozen pond with nowhere to hide.

When the light of dawn illuminated the statue, the old lion sat like a sentry, its dirty brownish-gray coloring intact. Actually, I thought the statue needed a new coat of paint, but as I recall the incident, perhaps black and orange weren't really good choices anyway. One fraternity brother told us the local police had been informed the statue had been targeted for a fresh coat of paint and to be on the lookout for vandals on the prowl. We did wonder why there was a police car parked in the area well into the wee hours of the morning. Needless to say, with the glow of the morning sunrise off in the distance and the police car still parked nearby, we abandoned the task. Although we didn't fulfill that obligation, the four candidates were initiated as new fraternity brothers of Kappa Theta!

NMHU: 1950 Drama Class Operetta

THE FBI

During the late 1940s and throughout the early 1950s, Senator Joseph McCarthy went on a rampage to purge communists and communist activities wherever they posed a threat to democracy and the American way of life. This purge included Hawai'i.

As a student at the University of Hawai'i during the fall semester of 1950, I was invited to attend what I thought was a student rally where food and soft drinks would be served. What probably got me interested in attending this rally was an attractive young woman, also a student at the university, who was distributing fliers about the rally. She was young, friendly, and about the same age as I was, twenty-one years old. It was easy to discuss anything with her. She seemed well versed on current events, not only in Hawai'i but also around the world. During those early years of my youth, I was bashful, not very talkative, and certainly not outspoken or demonstrative. Another reason for my interest in this meeting was the fact that food and beverages (nonalcoholic) would be available at no charge to those who attended.

I did manage to find the time to attend one meeting that basically expounded on the attributes of the United State of America and how lucky we were to be living in this country.

Although not apparent to me at that moment, after a few years had passed and I thought about what was said that night, there was an overtone of how the younger generation, the future leaders of

America, could improve the lives of everyone, especially those living in Hawai'i. Basically, the discussion was generalized to make students aware of how they could help their country by questioning our government leaders and having them explain several things that should be answered.

The meeting was on the second floor of a two-story wooden structure in Waikiki, across the street from where the 'Ilikai Hotel now stands. I recall there was a huge mango tree in the parking lot. After parking my car and entering the room where the meeting was being conducted, the young lady who handed me the flier at the university welcomed me into the room. She even remembered my name: "Hi, Bill, so glad you could come. I know you'll enjoy the lecture." After a few more words, she added, "Please take a seat anywhere, but you might want to sit near the lectern so the speaker can hear your questions if you need to have him explain something you don't understand."

A few days later, my sister asked if I had been to a student rally in Waikiki. I told her I was there around seven o'clock on a Tuesday night. She asked me if I knew the FBI had been watching the group that organized the meeting. That, I didn't know. An FBI agent she had been dating told her, "We saw your brother at the meeting." He suggested she tell me to "stay away from those people." The group had been tagged as a recruiting agency for the Communist Party. "Their approach," he told my sister, "is deemed detrimental to the United States; the FBI is tracking their activities at these meetings." After my sister told me about the FBI warning, I knew I wouldn't have any trouble staying away from that group. The lecture that night was so boring I knew I wouldn't be going back to that place again! However, meeting and talking to the very attractive female who remembered me, and gorging myself with sandwiches and soft drinks, well, that was the only good part of that meeting.

COSA NOSTRA, THE FBI, AND MY SISTER

· · · · · · · ● ● ● ● ● ● ● · · · · ·

During the early 1950s, the FBI was investigating Cosa Nostra, a well-organized criminal group that had control of gambling, prostitution, and other crimes related to underworld activities in the United States, particularly in the Chicago area.

During the summer of 1950, my sister, Carolyn, had applied for a job with Robinson Tours, a company owned by a family friend, Mary Robinson. This was my sister's first job in the field of tourism, and as a condition for being hired, Mary Robinson told her that a group of tourists would be arriving from Chicago the next day and if she could handle the group with little or no direction from the office, she would be hired on a permanent basis. In less than one day, my sister had to learn the fundamentals of what it was like to be a tour guide. The challenge was on!

The next day, when the United Airlines nonstop flight from Chicago arrived at Honolulu International Airport, only half of the group showed up. My sister expected six passengers but was surprised when only three women arrived. They told her their husbands would be arriving on a later f light from Chicago via Denver. Taking her three charges to the Royal Hawaiian Hotel to get them settled, my sister returned to the airport to meet their husbands. Upon retrieving their luggage, she had the taxi driver take them to meet their wives at the hotel.

Realizing the f lights from Chicago were long and tedious, my sister suggested everyone relax on the beach to get a feel for island life until the next day. Because of the time difference, it was suggested she meet them at seven o'clock (eleven o'clock Chicago time) the next morning for breakfast at the hotel to discuss a program plan that might be of interest to the group.

Because the men wanted to see Pearl Harbor, where the USS *Arizona* had been bombed, strafed, and sunk during the Japanese attack on December 7, 1941, my sister started their tour there. To the men this was an impressive sight; all were veterans of World War II, having served in European campaigns. The battles in the Pacific were a part of history they had not encountered. Throughout the rest of the week, the group was exposed to attractions such as a trip around the island, a luau, and a view of Honolulu from Punchbowl Crater, which had been converted into a cemetery for those who had been killed during World War II. The tour continued to the Pali lookout to view the windward side of O'ahu.

As an added attraction, my sister recommended trips to the island of Hawai'i to see Kilauea volcano and to Kaua'i where the group would see Waimea Canyon, the "Grand Canyon of the Pacific." The group thought that would be great, but because my sister lacked the experience to continue as their guide, she would transfer them to a more experienced tour operator. With that statement, the leader of the group immediately asked to see the owner of the travel agency. Upon finishing his conversation with Mary Robinson, my sister was told the group didn't want any other tour guide and that the group would pay all expenses to have her continue as their personal guide throughout their stay in Hawai'i. With that request, my sister's job with Mary Robinson Tours was firmly established.

On one occasion, while waiting with the women in the hotel's cocktail lounge for their husbands to join them, a purse that belonged to one of the women slipped from the bar counter and fell to the floor. Retrieving the purse for her client, my sister noticed a small handgun inside the purse. Her client said very casually, "We all carry handguns as protection against anyone who might want to harm us."

Further explanation revealed that the wives and husbands always traveled separately. They took this precaution because if something drastic happened to their husbands, the wives would be available to take care of the children. My sister told me she thought this was a reasonable arrangement.

While traveling with this group during the two weeks, my sister got to know the three couples well and thought they were very pleasant, courteous, and actually a lot of fun. After seeing the women off on their nonstop f light to Chicago, she stayed with the men until they boarded their flight to Chicago via Los Angeles. One of the men shook my sister's hand, thanking her profusely for a wonderful visit to Honolulu and the other islands. As their hands released, my sister was surprised to see a one-hundred-dollar bill in the palm of her right hand. He winked at her and said the group really enjoyed their trip to Hawai'i; they had a great time.

Several days after the group left Honolulu, FBI agents approached my sister and asked if she would testify against these men. During her interrogation by the FBI, she was informed that these men were part of an ongoing investigation of Cosa Nostra criminal activities. My sister declared that while in contact with this group, they treated her exceptionally well. Their activities were confined to the scenic beauty of the islands, its people, and the culture, nothing more. She flatly refused to make false statements merely to satisfy the FBI.

MILITARY REVIEW BOARD

In February 1951, when I enlisted in the army during the Korean conflict, I volunteered my services for the OCS (Officer Candidate School). As a requirement, all potential candidates had to be approved by a review board comprised of military officers. At an appointed time and place, I awaited my turn for an interview with other candidates; I was the final candidate for that day. A sergeant approached me and told me to enter the room where interviews were being conducted.

Upon entering the room, I was instructed to close the door and have a seat. Facing me were five officers. In descending order there was a colonel, a major, two captains, and a first lieutenant. After they introduced themselves to me, I was asked my name, where I lived, and what school I attended. After these social amenities were completed, the fireworks erupted!

Several times during the twenty-minute interview, the panel members simultaneously asked questions on different subjects. It was obvious I couldn't answer all the questions immediately but did manage to make my replies to each question, one at a time, in the order they were asked. After leaving the room and thinking about their method of questioning, I came to what seemed to be a logical conclusion. They were testing my reaction while "under fire."

One question asked was "Why are you applying for infantry?" When that question arose, the entire panel remained silent waiting to hear my reply. I'm sure they were interested to learn why anyone in his or her right mind would even think of volunteering for the infantry when a war was raging in Korea. My answer was a simple one. As a student at Kamehameha School, the ROTC program was directed toward basic infantry training. When asked what rank I held as a cadet, my reply was second lieutenant, responsible for leading a platoon of cadets through basic drills and mock battles.

Two weeks later I received a letter of acceptance as a candidate for officer training. The letter instructed me to report to Schofield Barracks for initial orientation. From there I would be sent to Fort Ord, California, for fourteen weeks of basic training followed by two weeks of command school. From Fort Ord I would be transferred to Fort Benning, Georgia, for three months and upon successfully completing the training at Fort Benning, I would be commissioned as a second lieutenant. The entire program for potential second lieutenants took three months. I'm sure this is how the term "ninety-day wonder" was coined.

Newly commissioned officers were being shipped to Korea. I wasn't surprised that, because of their lack of experience in a war zone, second lieutenants were rapidly put out of commission, so the army needed replacements as soon as possible.

MY ONE AND ONLY BLIND DATE

· · · · · · · ●●● ● ●●● · · · · · ·

With a passion I hated blind dates, but I got suckered into this one and what a whopper it was!

It all started one evening when I got a call from a cousin of a girl I had dated when I was enrolled at New Mexico Highlands University in Las Vegas, New Mexico, a small college town with a population of about fifteen thousand people, just sixty-five miles from Santa Fe and about 130 miles from New Mexico's largest city, Albuquerque. My girlfriend had moved to El Cajon, California, and had written to her cousin, Joe Sanchez, suggesting he and I get together. Joe was stationed at Pearl Harbor.

We did get together a few times when he was off the base, often meeting at a local bar or dance hall in downtown Honolulu. This time his call was a little different. He asked if I would do a double date.

"Hell's bells," I told him, "I hate blind dates! Why don't you get one of your navy buddies?"

"I couldn't find anyone who could get off from a Wednesday night duty," he replied. "Bill, I'm really desperate."

Joe proceeded to tell me how he had been trying to date this cute WAVE, but she wouldn't go out with him unless it was a double date. She always made excuses, but this time not only had he found another WAVE to go on the double date, he also managed to get someone to stand her watch the night he arranged the date. I told myself if Joe went through all this trouble, he must be desperate. Reticent to the idea but feeling sorry for Joe, I agreed to be a party to his scheme. His pigeon, yours truly, was cooped! I did promise I would help him if he really and truly couldn't find anyone else.

Since I didn't have a base pass, I volunteered to pick up the trio at Pearl Harbor's main gate. Joe asked if I would suggest a nice place where we could enjoy an evening of dining and dancing, a place where he could impress his date. I recommended a popular nightclub called Queen's Surf on Waikiki Beach, a place where I thought the food was good, the service was excellent, and best of all, there was a dance band. I also mentioned to Joe that I knew the bandleader, Sterling Mossman, and most of his musicians. Joe thought that was great so I made reservations for four.

At the appointed hour, Joe and his two companions were at the Pearl Harbor main gate waiting for me. After stepping out of the car, Joe introduced me to his date and then introduced me to Shawn, my date for the evening, a tall (five foot seven), attractive blonde. She wore a dark blue cocktail dress, a good contrast to her beautiful complexion. She was gorgeous! Joe had outdone himself. As a blind date, I thought my partner was a lot cuter than his. Opening the door on the passenger side, Joe and his date crawled into the backseat. I then invited Shawn to join me in the front seat. She seemed a bit shy, but we did have a nice get-to-know-each-other chat during our ten-mile drive from Pearl Harbor to Waikiki. Glancing in the rearview mirror, I could see Joe wasn't wasting any time. He had snuggled so close to his date I thought there was only one person in the backseat.

Stopping at the main entrance of the nightclub, Joe and the girls stepped out of the vehicle and waited while I parked the car. We approached the dining room where I mentioned my name and the reservations I had made for our group. The maître 'd started to lead us to a table a few rows away from the dance floor. Seeing me enter the door, the bandleader got the attention of the maître 'd and pointed to the empty table in front of the band. It appeared to Joe and the two girls that we were being treated as special guests of the club. Getting a table just off the dance floor made quite an impression on the trio. In my own way I wanted the evening to be a good one, especially for Joe and his date. After all, it was his party. When the bandleader, Sterling Mossman, finished the song they had been playing, I walked to the bandstand to thank him for the VIP treatment and to say hi to the other musicians. Upon returning to our table, Joe gave me a sly nod of appreciation for furthering his quest to impress and conquer.

We had an excellent meal, and to work it off, we continued with cocktails and dancing. All was going well for Joe, but when he asked my date, Shawn, for a dance, that's when the roof caved in. To complete the scenario, I reciprocated by asking his date if she wanted to dance to which she promptly replied, "Not really!" Her quick response gave me a feeling of rejection and that she wasn't enjoying the company or the event, so I tested the issue by asking her if she would like to take a walk around the club grounds. To my surprise, she said, "Yes!" We chatted as we walked on the pathway adjacent to the beach when suddenly, without a word, she stopped and took her shoes off and handed them to me. Lifting her dress above her knees, she walked to the water's edge where she watched the water curling around her ankles as the waves rushed up the sandy beach. Gently kicking the warm ocean water, she moved forward. She seemed happy. This, of course, pleased me because I felt I was contributing to Joe's desire to make sure his date was having a good time. Grasping her hand, I helped her up from the beach onto the grassy embankment and back onto the pathway. Holding my hand, she put on her shoes, and without releasing her hand from mine, we continued to walk and talk. I was encouraged and flattered. My fears of rejection were unfounded.

The moonlight filtering through the coconut trees, its leaves casting a shimmering shadow that danced along the garden path, and the soothing Hawaiian music from the band all added to the making of a very romantic setting, much like scenes pictured on postcards showing Waikiki Beach on moonlit nights.

Twenty minutes later we returned to our table only to be met by a silent, fuming Joe. The glaring look from my date was a killer, and from the way Joe looked at me, I could tell he was saying, "Bill, you're dead meat!" With nothing else to say, we left the nightclub. No one uttered a word during our ride back to the base. Earlier I said I hated blind dates, but in this case, it was the one and only blind date I really enjoyed! I married Joe's date, Theresa Sharretts Lindsay, personnelman third class, USN, exactly four months to the day after we met on that eventful evening, Wednesday, April 16, 1952.

Saturday, August 16, 1952

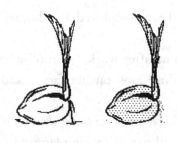

THE COCONUT WIRELESS

· · · · · · ● ● ● ● ● ● ● · · · ·

One form of communication in Hawai'i is what residents call "the coconut wireless." Often when asked, "How did you know that?" the reply would be "I heard it on the coconut wireless." There's no mystique in this communication; it's just another way of asking, "What's the latest gossip?"

On a warm July evening in 1952, as my fiancée and I sat on a park bench in Waikiki watching the ocean waves lazily lapping up and down the sandy shore, we mutually decided we wanted to spend our lives together in matrimonial bliss. The first step toward this goal was to meet at nine o'clock the next morning when the Bureau of Licenses, Department of Vital Statistics, Territory of Hawai'i, opened its doors. At the carefree age of twenty-three, this was our decision; we certainly didn't need an approval, confirmation, opinion, or review from anyone else.

My fiancée requested a few hours of leave time from her assigned workstation at Pearl Harbor that morning to meet me at the designated office. Once the forms were completed, we lovingly entwined our hands, shyly looking at each other, happy as larks. We were just two people reveling in happiness, knowing we had taken the first step toward years of married life, happily in love. This was what we wanted to do, forever sharing our lives together.

My fiancée returned to her duty station at Pearl Harbor (she was a WAVE); I went back to my desk in the attorney general's office at

'Iolani Palace, where I was employed as a library clerk assisting five attorneys.

Upon arriving home after work, my mother met me at the door, and with a reprimanding look on her face asked, "Who is this girl you're marrying?"

I thought, "*How the heck does she know about that?*"

"Why didn't you tell me you were planning to get married?" my mother asked.

Again I thought to myself, "*How did she know about this? My fiancée and I made that decision last night!*"

"Leila Rankin called me and said you applied for a license to get married," my mother declared.

Once again, I thought, "*Who the heck is Leila Rankin?*"

My question was immediately answered when my mother said, "*Your cousin helped you fill out the papers!*"

No wonder the clerk kept looking at me, asking if my mother's name was Lydia Wright and my father was William Wright. She even repeated the home address on the application. I remember thinking she must be checking the information written on the forms to be sure they were accurately recorded. It was then I realized the clerk just wanted to be sure she would be talking to the right person when she started the coconut wireless.

Three weeks later we had a beautiful ceremony, but during those three weeks, friends and relatives would say, "I hear you're getting married" or "I hear you're taking the big step" or "Who's the lucky girl?" This was amazing, absolutely amazing! I didn't tell anyone about getting married; my fiancée really didn't know any of my friends or relatives so I knew she didn't spread the word about our decision to tie the knot.

We spent our honeymoon on the windward side of O'ahu at a small cottage hidden among tropical plants and ironwood trees; it was a gorgeous place to swim and bask in the sun. The next morning, shedding our PJs for swimming suits, we splashed our way into the warm ocean, frolicking, laughing, and teasing each other. Just fifty feet from us taking their morning swim was another couple.

Moving toward us was a relatively attractive woman, several years older than me, and when she was only twenty feet away, she excitedly called, "Billy! How are you?"

Putting her mouth close to my ear, my wife whispered, "Who's that?"

Turning to her, I very quietly said, "Emma Blake."

"Who is that?" my wife asked.

"A relative," I replied.

Whispering in my ear she said, "Only four of us in this huge ocean and one is a relative?"

As my cousin swam up to us, she said, "I heard you were getting married. So this is your wife?"

Before I could make an introduction, she added, "You must be Tess! We heard Billy was getting married. I'm Billy's cousin! I'm so pleased to meet you."

After a bit of light conversation, we parted company. My cousin swam off to her partner while we headed for the beach. As we lay on the warm sand, my wife asked, "How did she know my name?"

"Well," I replied, "that's Hawai'i's coconut wireless when it started with the clerk who helped us complete the marriage license!"

DIANE

I'm sure we've all done things that seem to be exciting, adventurous, thrilling, and daring. In mid-August 1955, a hurricane designated "Connie" had come and gone, but in less than a week, there was "Diane" rapping at our door; another hurricane was bashing its way along the Atlantic seaboard onto the Carolina coastline, steadily moving northward. This hurricane was expected to veer inland and slam into Maryland and Delaware.

From Ocean City, Maryland, to Rehoboth Beach, Delaware, lies a long, beautiful, white sandy beach, and in between these two summer resort towns is a smaller village, Bethany Beach, a little Delaware township where my wife's cousin had her summer cottage.

About 150 miles inland from Maryland's shoreline is Baltimore and a suburb called Catonsville, where we had established our residency. For several days the *Baltimore Sun*, our local newspaper, had tracked Connie and was now tracking Diane. Hurricane Connie had kicked up some hefty winds and dumped a lot of water that created an Olympic-sized swimming pool in our backyard. Television newscasters were keeping an anxious eye on Diane's development and the path it was expected to take. From what was being said, it was possible that Hurricane Diane could be worse than Connie.

With a spirit of adventure luring us into the unknown, my wife and I said to each other, "Let's see for ourselves just exactly what a hurricane does when it smashes into Ocean City." We wanted to feel the force of the wind and rain as it hit our faces; we wanted to experience these forces of nature that only a hurricane can generate ... so twelve hours before Hurricane Diane was expected to reach Maryland's shoreline, we hopped in our car and drove eastward toward Ocean City, Maryland. We left Catonsville around 6:00 a.m.

The fastest, most direct route between Baltimore and Ocean City is via US Route 50, generally four hours of driving time from our home in Catonsville. Making the drive in three and a half hours was exceptional. On this trip, however, it took us nearly six hours to reach our destination. Although the traffic was going in the opposite direction, all intersections were jammed, which caused a long delay in traffic movement. Making an inane comment to my wife sitting next to me, I said, "Look at all the cars going away from Ocean City!" One might say I had a grasp for the obvious! For both of us, at twenty-six years of age, this was a second-childhood experience. We were young, filled with exhilaration and excitement. We had a very memorable and unforgettable adventure that has remained implanted in my mind, all because of that one day during the last week of August in 1955.

When we reached Ocean City, the wind velocity and rain was so powerful we had to travel at a snail's pace on the main thoroughfare, a four-lane, undivided highway running parallel to the beach just two blocks from the Atlantic Ocean. We saw no vehicles in the area; we had the entire city to ourselves. Our car was the only moving vehicle in that town. Because the wind was blowing white sand from the beach, it appeared as though a coating of snow had just fallen on the road. The torrential downpour was so heavy the wipers couldn't keep the windshield clear, and as the wind buffeted the car, we weaved unsteadily. This was not a good situation, so we decided to get out of Ocean City and drive north toward Bethany Beach, Delaware, a driving time of about twenty-five minutes. It took us nearly an hour to get to the summer cottage owned by my wife's cousin, a cottage built on the beach. No one was home. We parked the car on the leeward side of the cottage, and although the wind and rain kept swirling around us, we were somewhat sheltered by the sand dune between the cottage and the ocean. We walked around the cottage facing the beach. The force of the wind, the rain, the sand, the ocean spray, and the rising surf pounding its way to the front door of the cottage seemed exhilarating. As each wave crested the sand dune, debris rushed past us stopping just short of the cottage door. Suddenly, we heard something smashing into the cottage. A small flat piece of plywood with jagged splinters hit the corner of the cottage just behind us. My wife and I looked at each other and, without a word, moved back to the sheltered side of the house and into our car. This was not a good time to be visiting relatives in Delaware.

We drove northward on a highway running parallel to the beach. The sand dunes between the ocean and the main road did provide some protection from the wind. Upon reaching the resort town of Rehoboth Beach, we turned west and headed home.

It took us six hours to get to the seashore, an hour and a half to cruise the coastline highway, five minutes to spend on the beach, and just two seconds to say, "Let's get out of this place!" With little traffic impeding our trip home, it took us five hours to return to Catonsville. Once inside our cozy apartment, we felt safe and secure. The pelting rain was just another heavy downpour refilling our recently created backyard swimming pool.

Was it exhilarating? Was it fascinating? Was it wonderful? A resounding yes to all of these questions! Would I do it again? I don't think so. Driving into a hurricane to experience the forces of nature just to satisfy one's curiosity was not a bright idea. We were young and very, very stupid.

INNOCENCE OF THE YOUNG

· · · · · · ●●● ● ●●● · · · · ·

In the mid-1950s Art Linkletter had a television show that featured children to whom he asked leading questions about their lives with Mommy and Daddy. With childlike innocence, their answers were often entertaining.

We lived in Maryland in a small community called Glen Burnie, a suburb of Baltimore. During the summer months, the area can be hot and muggy, so to counter a hot day, we purchased a small wading pool ten feet in diameter that could be filled with water eighteen inches deep. My wife purchased new bathing suits for the girls, and on one of those hot summer days, she dressed them in their new swimwear so they could cool off by splashing and frolicking in the wading pool. One daughter, Kappy, was 2½ years old; the other, Lani, was 3½ years old.

The first time we let the girls use their new wading pool the telephone rang. From the back bedroom, my wife said, "Bill, you answer the phone!"

"Hello?" I asked.

"Do you know your children don't have any clothes on?" the caller stammered.

Looking through the kitchen window, I could see my children had taken off their bathing suits and placed them a few feet away from the pool. They seemed very much at home splashing each other on that warm summer day. Walking into the kitchen, my wife silently mouthed, "Who's that?" With the telephone still pressed to my ear, I pointed to our neighbor's house across the backyard. In another silent conversation, my wife asked, "What does she want?" This time I pointed to the two girls standing in the pool, and as we watched, they waved to their mommy and daddy looking out the kitchen window.

Having been informed our children wore no bathing suits and having confirmed this fact, I politely thanked our neighbor for her observation. After cradling the telephone, my wife and I went into hysterical laughter. Since our daughters were only 2½ and 3½ years old, we were not about to reprimand them or insist they put on their swimsuits while they were thoroughly enjoying themselves. It was apparent to us that we had a neighbor who seemed offended we would allow our toddlers to swim without bathing suits. Did this mean we had to stop the children from cooling off in the wading pool that hot summer day? Certainly not!

When the girls were tired of playing in the pool and had entered the house, both had put on their bathing suits. When they were inside, I casually asked, "Why did you take off your bathing suits?"

What seemed to be a logical answer, Lani, our 3½-year-old daughter replied, "We didn't want to get our new clothes wet!"

THE STORM, WAS IT A DREAM?

· · · · · · · ● ● ● ● ● · · · · ·

It was 3:00 a.m. in Maryland. I was sound asleep and suddenly felt the wind and rain blowing through the screen above our bed. Water was splashing on my face; I was getting drenched from the heavy rain. This, of course, awakened me, and as I sleepily jumped out of bed to close the window, I noticed a bright moon, its light shining through the window, with no clouds in the sky and only a few stars twinkling. "That's odd," I said to myself, "why did I feel rain was coming through the bedroom window?" Running my hand across my face, I expected it to be wet. It wasn't. Was this just a dream? If it was a dream, why did it seem so real? Reviewing the dream, I visualized a torrential downpour, a gale force wind blowing rain into the bedroom, and everything around me getting wet—the bedding, the clothes in the closet, the bureau, the floor!

With slippers on my feet, I walked into the living room, opened the front door, and stepped outside a few yards onto a dry walkway. I looked up and saw a bright moon, twinkling stars, and no storm clouds in the sky. In a daze I shuffled back into the house, shaking my head in wonderment. Upon entering the bedroom, I looked at the windowpane: not a drop of rain on it. Again I looked out the window; there was that bright moon, the stars twinkling, and no clouds. Still in awe, I crawled back into bed and soon fell into a deep sleep. The date was October 12, 1960.

Two years later, August 1962, I had an opportunity to visit Honolulu and see what changes had taken place during the ten years since settling in Maryland. My parents had moved from Waikiki to live in a quiet town on the opposite side of the island, a place called Kailua, far away from chattering tourists. They bought a large five-bedroom house on beachfront property where the white sandy beach stretched a mile in one direction and half a mile in the other direction.

Since this was my first time seeing their new home, my mother was eager to show me the house. On the ground floor there was a foyer that led into a large living room. Directly ahead was a staircase leading to the bedrooms. To the left of the foyer was a formal dining room and beyond that was a large kitchen. To the right of the foyer was a full-size bedroom complete with a private bathroom. This was to be my bedroom during my visit.

At the top of the stairs was a window overlooking the front lawn and the ocean. It was a beautiful scene, very tropical and majestic. On the right was a small bedroom with a standard double bed. A bathroom divided it from a second bedroom on the same side of the house. To my left was a large bedroom with twin beds and a shared bathroom with another bedroom on that side of the house. Turning around, away from the ocean, and walking down the hall to see the second bedroom, I entered it and audibly said, "This is the room!" My mother, with a quizzical look on her face, asked, "What did you say?" I told her about the dream I'd had two years earlier, that I felt rain pouring through the window drenching the curtains, wind blowing the rain across the room to the opposite side where the closet was located, and the bedroom floor drenched from the rain blowing through the windows. "That's right," my mother said. She then proceeded to tell me about that awful night. The more she told me about that storm, the more I was convinced my spirit was in that room experiencing the wind, the rain, and the water pouring in through the window—two years earlier, in 1960, five thousand miles away!

THERESA SHARRETTS LINDSAY

(June 7, 1929 – June 29, 1963)

She was always smiling and laughing, and had a zest for life, a wonderful sense of humor, and bright, twinkling eyes that often made her appear mischievously elfish. Yet, when she showed concern for others, it was with great wisdom and compassion only a loving and caring person could give.

As her eyes looked up searching and finding mine upon hers, she whispered softly and tenderly, "I love you." And as her eyes slowly closed, she leaned against my body, her fingers entwined with mine, gently squeezing until there was no strength left in them. It was then I knew she had entered a new life in an unknown world.

Springing into action, I instructed Lani, my ten-year-old daughter, to pick up the telephone. How it was that I came to know the numbers as I rattled them off to her still puzzles me, for never had I been able to call our family physician without first looking for his number in the telephone directory. In a state of panic, I dashed from the phone to my wife, unerringly following his precise instructions. After several agonizing minutes that seemed like hours, I realized the futility of continuing. With a heavy heart, tears clouding my vision, I groped along the wall to replace the telephone onto its holder.

The medical team arrived, and as I watched their frantic efforts through tear-stained eyes, I saw the look of helplessness pass from one to the other. Their frustration must have been as great as mine. Slowly they rose and quietly packed their medical kits. As they passed me to leave, one of them paused, put his left hand gently on my left shoulder, and said, "I'm sorry, there's nothing more we can do."

The house was empty; all was quiet as though the stillness of night had fallen. The silence was deafening. In silent anger and frustration, I screamed, "Oh God, why? What have I done to deserve this? If it must be so, why not me? The girls need their mother! Please, dear God, bring her back! Tell me it's not true! What will I say to the children? How can I tell them what has happened? Oh God, why her? Why not me? Please, dear God, *help* me!"

Many years have passed since that fateful morning, June 29, 1963, and when I look back to reflect upon the good times we shared, those moments of happiness still remain a part of me. I can only wish she was with me to share my joy and delight when I watched our children chasing butterflies, building sandcastles on the seashore, kicking autumn leaves, and tossing snowballs at trees barren of leaves. I can only hope that through my eyes, she, too, saw the delight we should have been sharing together.

Someday, perhaps, in the not-too-distant future, we will meet again—in her world!

THE GRAVEYARD SHIFT

I may not be the brightest person, and if you've taken the time to read some of my stories, you already know I've done a lot of stupid things. However, I really think this short story should take the proverbial cake!

Most winters in Maryland aren't really too bad, but there are times when a brisk wind can take a twenty-eight-degree temperature and create a wind-chill factor of something close to zero degrees.

On a cold January night after a late session at work, my good friend John Coviello and I decided to have a drink to unwind. We thought that Dino's, one of our favorite watering holes, would be a good place to meet. Dino's was a restaurant located in Glen Burnie, a small town half-way between Baltimore and Annapolis, Maryland. When we worked overtime hours, which took us well past nine o'clock at night, we often stopped at Dino's to have a few drinks and discuss the progress on our projects before heading home to our respective residences. On this very cold and blustery January night, we stayed at Dino's a little longer than usual and left only because Maryland laws prohibited local pubs from keeping their doors open after 2:00 a.m.

As we left the restaurant, the cold wind forced us to wrap our overcoats around our bodies to keep from freezing. The waitresses who had been serving us had also completed their evening shift and stepped outside with us. After a brief chat with the waitresses, John and I left Dino's with the understanding that I would stop at his house in Catonsville for a few cups of coffee to discuss our progress on the project. As I drove up to the front of John's house in Catonsville (around 2:30 a.m.), Deweese, John's wife, ran out of the house demanding, "Where have you and John been?" Evidently, my wife, Alma, was on the telephone at that moment advising Deweese that the two husbands parted company with the waitresses and that she would be following the waitresses to see where they were going. The spot chosen by the waitresses was an all-night Chinese restaurant called The Rice Bowl, a place we sometimes frequented after pub hours. I must have looked rather perplexed because all I could say to Deweese was truthfully, "At Dino's. John should be right behind me."

While on the telephone talking to Deweese, Alma said she had parked her car in a graveyard across from Dino's and waited there for two hours checking to see what John and I would do after we left the restaurant (in that freezing weather?). Alma informed Deweese she would follow the waitresses to see if John and I would be meeting up with them. Sitting in a car for two hours, even if the car engine was keeping the driver warm, certainly must have made Alma very uncomfortable. Was this jealousy? Because of the near freezing temperature that night, I prefer to term this stakeout as being incredibly stupid!

THE SWEET TASTE OF A RIPE PINEAPPLE!

• • • • • • • • • • ● • • • • • • • • • •

Pineapples are really tasty when they're fully grown and picked fresh from the field. In May 1970, after living nearly twenty years in Maryland, I relocated to Hawai'i. Within a week and a half of my arrival, I was invited to a luau where pineapples were to be part of the decorations for the tables being set to serve 150 people. Two hours before the guests arrived, a friend asked if I wanted to help pick pineapples from Dole's pineapple fields. Of course I was delighted to participate. A small Toyota pickup truck approached and three of us hopped onto the back. Off we went to Dole's prized fields on O'ahu.

Within fifteen minutes, nearing a dirt road blocked by a heavy chain, the passenger sitting in the cab jumped out of the truck, took a key from his pocket, and unlocked the padlock securing the chain. With the chain on the ground, the driver drove the pickup over it and waited for the passenger to stretch the chain and relock it. The dirt road was on the property of the sugar company, an access road into the sugarcane fields. As a foreman working for Waipahu Sugar Company, he had a key to unlock all the road chains in the sugarcane fields.

A mile beyond the cane field, rows of pineapples were visible emerging above their stalks. At various locations signs were posted warning people there would be a fine of twenty-five dollars for every pineapple taken from the field without authorization. Believing this was merely a formality, we continued to drive another mile or so. At one location one of the men in back of the Toyota pounded his hand on the top of the cab signaling the driver to stop. We all jumped out, and my friend pointed to the field where we would be picking the pineapples. The pineapples looked awfully small. I thought he was kidding because the pineapples in the next field were huge and certainly looked ripe. When I asked why we weren't going after the big ones, he replied, "Those are first crop; the ones we want are third crop, or fourth crop if we can find them."

Realizing how slow I was in selecting the pineapples to be picked, my friend said, "Hey, Bill, stand here!" With his left index finger pointing to a dirt road five hundred yards away, he said, "If you see a truck heading this way, tell us, okay?"

"Holy mackerel," I muttered to myself, "these guys are stealing the pineapples! Here I am back in Hawai'i less than two weeks and I'm going to jail!" I counted thirty pineapples in the pickup truck, and at twenty-five dollars a shot, that was $750!

We didn't land in jail, and we didn't pay any fine; we did, however, eat the sweetest, juiciest pineapples I have ever tasted!

THE IDES OF MARCH

• • • • • • ● ● ● ● ● ● • • • •

Approaching our apartment in Baltimore on a late afternoon, my wife, Alma, opened the door and said, "Your sister called from Honolulu an hour ago. She wants you to call her as soon as possible."

With a nod, I went to the telephone and after a few rings, my mother answered, "Hello?"

"Carolyn left a message for me to call her," I said. "Is she there?"

I could hear my mother sobbing. "Is anything wrong?" I asked.

There was no response from her, but a few seconds later my sister responded, "Dad is in the hospital; we took him there late this morning." After a few minutes of conversation, she said, "He's not expected to live through the night."

Upon cradling the telephone, my wife asked, "Is anything wrong?"

I looked up and sadly replied, "Yes, my father is in the hospital. Carolyn said he's not expected to live through the night."

Without saying a word, my wife went to the cupboard, pulled out a candle and candlestick holder, lit the candle, and placed it on our dining table in the kitchen. As the late afternoon wore on into evening, we sat at the table in quiet solitude. Our only light in the room came from the glowing candle. Our conversation, soft and reverent, seemed like a wake. My wife said, "He was like a father to me. He was always there when I needed someone to talk to."

The candle glowed with a steady stream of light, flickered, and then glowed. "My father is dying," I said.

"What do you mean?" she asked.

I replied, "Did you notice the candle flicker?"

"Yes," she responded.

During the next hour, the candlelight f lickered several times. I looked around the room; the windows were closed. I got up from my chair and walked to the front door to feel if there was a draft coming through the door. There wasn't. I walked to the back door. It, too, was closed. For several seconds I stood in the foyer; there was no draft circulating throughout the apartment to cause the candlelight to flicker.

The candle continued to glow, dimmed, glowed, and again flickered. Suddenly, without warning, the room was engulfed in darkness. I said to my wife, "I think my father just died." It was 3:00 a.m. in Baltimore. My father died at 10:00 p.m. in Honolulu, five thousand miles away, on March 15, 1970.

BEACH PARTIES

Built on an acre of ground, my parents two-story house in Kailua was about two hundred feet from the ocean where a white sand beach stretched a half mile in one direction and a mile and a half in the opposite direction. At the shorter end was a barrier reef. At the other end, a rocky cliff stopped the beach from expanding farther. Like a good many people, I enjoy a beach party every once in a while but at midnight on dark nights? Well, I'm not sure this was an ideal time for a picnic. The gathering often occurred just outside the downstairs bedroom I occupied. Perhaps it was my luck to have that bedroom, or perhaps it was by design when my mother said I might like that particular room with its sliding door, which opened onto the front lawn facing the ocean. Because of the parties, some people would probably say my bedroom was a bit too noisy. Maybe so, but I did find an intense interest in the conversations on those dark noisy nights.

The first time I heard the voices was in August 1970, three months after leaving my job at Westinghouse in Linthicum, Maryland, a suburb of Baltimore. I had returned to Hawai'i to help my mother with the estate after my father died. I said to myself, "Why in the world would this group of laughing, joking people want to party in *our* yard at the corner of *our* house next to *my* bedroom?" Naturally, I got up to see what was going on. If you can't fight them, why not join them? At least that's what I thought as I opened the sliding door facing the beach. I stepped out onto the grassy lawn; the stars were somewhat obscured by the clouds moving inward from the ocean, and there was no moonlight, only a gentle breeze. Nary a soul did I see outside my bedroom. Stepping back through the sliding door into my bedroom, I said to myself, "I must have been dreaming!" I crawled back into my bed and promptly fell asleep.

Two months later there was another beach party; the laughing, talking, and joking were clearly audible to me. This time I lay awake listening to the voices and what they were saying. Unfortunately, the conversation was in Hawaiian, a native language I never did understand. Although I recognized a word here and there, my knowledge of the language was extremely limited. It seemed these parties always occurred on dark nights, always with a gentle breeze blowing inland.

Knowing an old-timer familiar with the area, I told him about the parties. He was surprised I heard the partygoers. The next time he visited us, I took him to where the voices always seemed the loudest, just outside my bedroom. Looking around the area, toward the beach, and back to the spot where we were standing, he made an interesting statement: "When I was five years old, my grandfather told me there used to be a path to the beach used by ancient Hawaiian fishing parties. I think this is the area where they gathered. You may have been hearing voices of the past, a gift not too many people have."

Whether this was true or not, I don't really know. My sister, who slept in that room before I occupied it, also heard those voices, always on dark nights.

THE PALI

· · · · · · · ●· · · · · · · ·

It was a late August night in 1970 when I left my office in Waikiki
to return home on the windward side of the island. A usual route
is the Old Pali road that climbs to about twelve hundred feet and
then continues downward with many curves and tight turns. About
two miles from the top of the Pali, I heard my father's voice yelling
my name, "Billy!" His voice, loud, sharp, and clearly audible, would
awaken anyone within hearing. I had fallen asleep at the wheel.
Suddenly, wide awake, I saw my father's stern face on the windshield
in front of me, glaring at me with that admonishing expression he
used when demanding attention. The car I was driving was drifting
toward the guardrail dividing the east-west lanes. My father had died
in March, five months earlier.

Having reached the Pali tunnel at the top of the mountain, I
started my downhill run, but right there in front of me was a man
riding a bicycle. I remember saying to myself, "No one in his right
mind should be riding a bicycle on the Pali road, especially at two
o'clock in the morning."

As I cautiously moved my car left to pass the cyclist, he blocked
my path. Because he was now in front and just to the left of my left
fender, I moved to the right to pass him. There he was again, right in
front of me. At the bottom of the hill, I stopped, looked up, and saw

the traffic signal separating the road—one to Kane'ohe, the other to Kailua—its red light staring at me. I had fallen asleep at the wheel but had been guided downhill by a cyclist who had mysteriously disappeared when I stopped at the traffic light!

WORLDS APART

In an earlier story, a kahuna was consulted to see what was wrong with my sister because she was unable to walk, yet nothing was found to be physically wrong. Let me relate a story involving the same kahuna, who worked on me. Before I continue, let me give you a little background as to why this kahuna was asked to see me.

During the summer of 1944, the same summer my sister had her experience with the kahuna of death, an incident occurred that is still vividly entrenched in my mind. For a growing boy of fifteen, not wanting to eat breakfast, lunch, dinner, candy, cookies, or other snacks; not wanting to go surfing; and always too tired to do anything except sleep all day and all night was definitely an abnormal situation. My aunt who lived next door became concerned when she noted my surfboard standing on its end against the house, unused, and never seeing me running around the yard playing with the other boys in the neighborhood.

With my mother's permission, my aunt consulted her friend, Mary, a kahuna. She asked Mary if she would visit me and explain why it seemed that I just wanted to sleep, was always very tired, and never wanted to eat anything.

On a late morning that summer, Mary arrived, and upon entering my bedroom, she noted I was in a very deep sleep. As I was being awakened, I drowsily remember Mary saying to my aunt how difficult it was to awaken me. "This is a very troubled boy who is being torn between two worlds," she said. Mary asked me to move from the single bed in my dark room to a double bed in another room, the same bed my sister used. The room had more windows and was brighter and airier. Having moved to the double bed, Mary asked me to lie on my stomach, which I did. She then proceeded to rub the calf of my left leg, gently massaging it, and gradually pressed harder and harder until her massaging felt like torture. Although I said nothing, I winced in pain when her massaging grew more intense. Suddenly, turning to my aunt who was standing nearby, Mary blurted, "Look, look, see the four dots on this boy's leg?" With a sense of curiosity, I turned my head and looked over my left shoulder to see what they saw. Mary was pointing to the four dots on the calf of my left leg, which I, too, saw.

As in the story relating to my sister's experience, Mary knew nothing about our family history, yet what she told my aunt was almost unbelievable.

"These four dots," Mary said, "are formed in the sign of a cross. When this boy was a baby, he lived with a family member who became so strongly attached she wanted to adopt him. I see this family member is not alive today, yet her love for this boy is so strong she is pulling him to join her. I also see that when he lived with this woman, this boy considered her to be his mother!"

A few months after I was born, my mother had become quite ill and could not take care of me. Traditionally, when this occurs, other family members will oversee the care and nurturing of a growing child. My mother's sister, who was several years older and helped my grandmother take care of younger siblings, volunteered to take that responsibility. For a year and half, although she had three daughters of her own, I was the boy she wanted, the son she never had.

She begged my mother to let her adopt me, a request my mother refused. When it was time for me to leave Honolulu and sail back to Kaua'i on the SS *Waialale*, one of two inter-island steamers that transported passengers between the major islands, I was told the parting was very difficult. Considering my aunt to be the only mother I knew, I was told I clung so hard to her shoulder that pieces of skin from her body got into my fingernails. In a similar manner, she wrapped her arms around me so tightly there was a blending of souls. It was with extreme effort that family members tore us apart! The scene, I was told, was not a pleasant one. The wailing cries of my aunt could be heard throughout the length of the pier, and my screams could be heard the entire length of the ship as it pulled away from the dock.

THE TRAVEL BUSINESS

My bed bounced lightly as though someone had sat down on it. As I sleepily rolled over to see who was rudely waking me, my sister, Carolyn, sitting on the lower left corner of the bed, said, "I got the feeling you're still interested in going into the travel business."

Stretching under the covers, propping my pillow, and cradling my hands under my head, I replied, "Yeah, I've been thinking about it a lot lately. We discussed this a while back just before I moved to Virginia in January 1977, remember?"

"I remember," she said. "Anyway, the reason I came to see you is to remind you what I told you about getting into the travel business and how tough it is to get a foot in the door when you're just starting."

Our conversation covered at least twenty minutes of discussion on the advantages and disadvantages of the travel business.

As my sister stood up, she said, "Gotta go now. Take my advice; don't even think about going into the travel business unless you can stand a negative cash flow for at least six months. Remember what I told you earlier: the airlines don't care who you are, just so they get their payments for the tickets you issue to your clients. You have to be sure the money is in the bank every Monday before noon. If you don't have enough funds to cover your ticket sales report, ASTA will close you down immediately. They won't give you a second chance." With that last comment, Carolyn left the room.

This conversation took place during the summer of 1989, ten years after my sister died. It may have been a dream, but because the sensation of a bouncing bed awakened me and I was having a conversation with a person sitting at the foot of my bed, all seemed real. Since that conversation, although I haven't given up the idea of starting a travel agency, my desire to pursue my ambition to get into the travel business was curbed.

PU'IWA

Date: March 21, 1996

Time: 9:22am (+/- 5min.)

Prelude: Collecting tax material for today's appointment with Income Tax Accountant Jessica Kraemer

Walked into bedroom to check if tax material might be in bureau drawers; strong odor of cigar smoke filled the room. No other room in this house has the odor of cigar smoke. No workers are outside. Immediately thought of my father who was a cigar smoker! Time: 9:34 a.m., cigar smoke odor has just drifted over my right shoulder as I am typing this note. Can this mean he is here to offer a guiding hand on my tax material?

Pu'iwa (pronounced "pooh-ee-va")—weird, ghostly feeling; bristling skin sensation; in colloquial slang, this is called "chicken skin"!

I WISH I DIDN'T, BUT WHAT'S DONE IS DONE!

'Twas forty-eight years ago
I stepped on a pedal, And away I did go
Pedal to the metal.
Heed my story of a midnight ride
And speeding on Interstate 5.

A bird flew by near San Clemente
A California Highway Patrol (CHP) Officer said,
"Speed you got aplenty!"
And for his efforts, on a whim,
A ticket was issued to "him."

And who is "him" we say?
Tell us now without delay!
"Ah," we answer with hilarious delight,
"'Twas none other than Willie Wright!"

The moral of this story is:
Don't, for goodness sakes alive,
Pass a CHP cruising at sixty-five
For surely you'll be remiss
When he clocks you doing seventy-six.

Our CHP was not too bright, that was evident.
He did not know how to ticket a Las Vegas resident.
But, alas, a speeding ticket Willie did get, to whit,
'Twas best served ignoring it!

STORIES MY FATHER TOLD ME

BACHELORHOOD ADVANTAGE

· · · · · · ●●●● ● ●●● · · · · ·

The island of Kaua'i is the fourth largest of seven inhabited islands in the Hawaiian Archipelago covering a landmass of about 553 square miles. Much of the island is mountainous terrain with many hidden valleys, wet mountain slopes, dense undergrowth, and a jungle of foliage, tall grasses, and trees.

In the early 1930s, prohibition was in full swing. Whiskey was difficult to obtain on the US mainland, not so on this small island with its population reaching a resounding 22,500 inhabitants.

As a bachelor, my father was known to have great parties, with lots to eat and drink. During those years of prohibition, getting whiskey never did present a problem. In Hawai'i it's not what you know, it's whom you know. His first call always went to a friend, Charlie Rice, who just happened to be the county sheriff.

"Hey, Charlie, this is Bill Wright; I'm having a party at my house next Saturday. I need some *okolehau*!"

"Come on, Bill, you know there's a prohibition on liquor. It's against the law to sell the stuff," the sheriff replied.

"Yeah, I know," my father said, "but the gang will be at the house this weekend. I invited Carolyn Wellis and asked her to bring a couple of other nurses from the hospital. She said she would be there with two friends."

"Will Mabel be there?" Charlie asked.

"Yeah, Carolyn said Mabel would be one of the nurses with her," my father replied.

"Okay!" Charlie said. "How much okolehau do you want?"

"Let's see, we have fifteen people showing up Saturday night. My brother George, Bill Akana, Bobby, and Moki will be at my place early to start a poker game. How about four gallons?" my father responded.

"You sure four gallons will be enough?" Charlie asked.

"Four gallons should be enough for this weekend," my father said.

"Okay! I'll get the whiskey tomorrow and deliver it Friday night," said Charlie.

RANK HAS ITS PRIVILEGES

My father was a cadet captain when he graduated from Kamehameha School for Boys in 1915, so he was given the rank of first lieutenant when he joined the Hawai'i National Guard. In Europe a war between Germany and the allies of Great Britain had been going on since 1914. Not until the United States sent its expeditionary force to Europe in 1917 did this war become "the war to end all wars," better known today as World War I.

Because the United States was now involved in this conflict, several National Guard units throughout the country were mobilized. The Hawai'i National Guard, now a part of the United States Army, was assigned to Fort Shafter, an army base located a few miles from downtown Honolulu. My father, as a first lieutenant with two years of service in the National Guard, was made a first lieutenant at Fort Shafter.

As an infantry officer, he would review newly inducted recruits and take them to Schofield Barracks for their basic infantry training. While reviewing a new group of inductees, he noticed a close friend in the group, and because officers were entitled to have aides, he instructed the sergeant reviewing the new recruits with him to assign one of them, Bill Akana, to be an officer's aide. No one knew that the person selected was from the same island where my father was born and raised, the island of Kaua'i. Being such close friends, my father would use his aide as a chauffeur for the car my father owned. Once past Fort Shafter's main gate, they would switch seats so my father would drive the car. Without bringing attention to themselves, both would shed their uniforms and slip into civilian attire. Most of those trips off base ended up at a local pub in downtown Honolulu.

From what my father told me, Bill Akana never did get any basic training, and because officer's aides usually held the rank of private first-class or corporal, my father was able to get corporal stripes for him.

Base housing was allotted according to rank, and because my father was the ranking first lieutenant, he was next in line to take the last remaining two-bedroom house on the base. Being a bachelor, my father had no need for a house, and because another first lieutenant with a wife and two children had recently arrived from San Francisco, he suggested the house be assigned to that family. My father requested accommodations at BOQ (bachelor officers' quarters) on the base.

BIOGRAPHICAL SKETCH

Bill Wright was born and raised in Hawai'i in a small sugar plantation town called Kekaha, on the hot dry side of Kaua'i. Entered as a boarding student at the Kamehameha School for Boys in August 1940, Bill graduated six years later and decided that working on a tugboat operating between Honolulu and the Pacific Northwest was more exciting than joining the army as a replacement for armed forces personnel released from duty following World War II. His last seafaring days started in Honolulu in early May 1948 and ended in Seattle twenty-nine days later. Infatuated with the green forests of Washington, its magnificent snow-capped Mount Rainier, and the warm, sunny days of late spring and summer, Bill decided to register as a student at the University of Washington but not for long; no one told him about the nine months of constant drizzle that followed those beautiful summer months.

At the outbreak of the Korean War, Bill volunteered for active service spending his entire tour of duty at Fort Ord, California.

A month after getting married in Honolulu (August 1952), Bill and his first wife, Theresa Sharretts Lindsay, moved to her hometown in Towson, Maryland, a suburb of Baltimore. Bill spent almost eighteen years with the Westinghouse Aerospace Division as a technical writer. Bill has two daughters, Beverly Kapualehuanani and Kathleen Pualani. Kappy, as family members call her, has one daughter, Kemelia, and Lani has two daughters, Kate, the younger of two, and Lindsay. One year after the death of his first wife, Bill married his second wife, Alma Boyd. "That marriage," Bill declared, "was not meant to be a lasting relationship." Following his divorce, Bill married his present wife, Gail, in May 1974 in Baltimore. He has two stepdaughters, Shelley Lynn (Fletcher) Temple and Angelica Renee Fletcher.

After almost eighteen years as an engineering writer working on military airborne fire-control systems at Westinghouse, Bill was hired as senior editor for DATA Books (a subsidiary of Mitchell Manuals, Inc.) in San Diego, California. When he resigned as senior editor, he decided to resume his education. At the ripe old age of fifty-two, Bill enrolled as a freshman at San Diego Miramar College and was academically recognized on the dean's list (1982–83) and in the prestigious *Who's Who in American Junior Colleges.* Bill received his associate's degree in business administration in June 1983.

Shortly after moving to San Diego in 1979, Bill became active in the Hui O Hawai'i of San Diego and the Hawaiian Interclub Council of Southern California (HICCSC), serving as an officer and board member of both clubs. Bill was also a member of Ahahui Kiwila O San Diego Hawaiian Civic Club with dual membership in the Las Vegas Hawaiian Civic Club, having served as a first vice president and recording secretary for LVHCC.

Hired by General Dynamics as a technical writer on the cruise missile project, Bill joined Rockwell International as a lead writer on the B-1 bomber program. After two and a half years, Bill resigned to start Innovative Consultants, Inc., a publications and data processing consulting firm located in Las Vegas, Nevada. Bill retired from publications and planned to write a biography of his life from the 1930s to the present day. Unfortunately, before this autobiography could be completed, Bill passed away on February 8, 2013. His wife, Gail, completed the book.

The Wright Family Home, Kekaha, Kaua'i
Craftsman house built in 1903 by Bill's father;
still in excellent condition today

Printed in the United States
By Bookmasters